THE

HEART-CENTERED

LEADER

PRAISE

"Jane acts from a place of humility, unconditional positive regard, and courage. She asks hard questions, she builds trust, she shows up with authenticity so, when it comes time for checking that everyone feels safe, people state their needs and experiences."
—Heidi van Rijswijk, educator and super coach

"Jane is a people and well-being first leader who builds trust through her genuine commitment to and care of the well-being of her staff. This isn't only evident in the way she connects and supports her staff on a personal and team level, but also in how she leads structural change to improve operations and culture to create psychologically safe and a prosperous workforce."
—Sally Cunningham, mother of two passionate about diversity and inclusion

"Jane is a pleasure to work with. She is extremely hardworking and has the smarts, as well as the natural warmth to develop trust and support all staff."
—Loretta Mannix-Fell, philanthropist guru

"Her high emotional intelligence can be seen in the biggest and smallest things she does every day. Jane is not afraid to admit a mistake, she will accept them and sees them as an opportunity for development and growth. Jane is not just an executive leader; Jane is my role model in my professional and personal life."
—Valentina Mozetic, HR professional and rescuer of animals

"Jane tackles challenges thoughtfully and with clear determination while also maintaining a level of kindness and consideration that I personally have not witnessed in an executive leader prior to working here. Her leadership style encourages team members to bring their best selves to work and encourages them to express their ideas openly, as Jane has worked to create a culture of safety, transparency and cooperation that enables this."
—Bella Moginie, organizational psychologist who loves to surf

PRAISE

"Jane exemplifies heart-centered leadership. She brings people together with purpose, creates safe and empowering spaces for collaboration, and turns complex challenges into shared breakthroughs. Through her guidance, I not only gained confidence in analysis and business improvement but also witnessed how exceptional leadership transforms teams and outcomes."
—Troy Robbins, a politically savvy, great human being

"I had the privilege of working with Jane who is a truly a heart-centered leader. Jane is someone who leads with empathy, authenticity, and a deep commitment to uplifting others around her. She's also wonderfully warm, intelligent, and offers a rare mix of strategy and pragmatism."
—Erin Freeman, heart-centered HR mastermind

"In this book, Jane discusses the concept of heartfelt leadership, emphasizing the importance of leadership that fosters enthusiasm among employees and creates an enviable workplace. Jane superbly shares her moving life story, and others' life experiences, whilst providing practical tools to help cultivate a peaceful work environment and promote accountability and the ability to engage in difficult conversations. The essence of effective leadership has been portrayed as demonstrating trust, self-improvement, and building strong relationships, ultimately guiding individuals to become extraordinary leaders. A book that is a must read for developing leaders."
—Pauline White, retired project professional and expert motorhome driver

"This book will make you deeply reflect on your own leadership style. Jane generously shares her story and those of others to beautifully demonstrate what leadership from the heart looks like and how it can have a ripple effect on those around you. For those of you already leading with your heart, it will validate and strengthen your resolve to have a positive impact on everyone you work with. And for others it will provide you the courage, the framework and the practical steps to make a positive change. After reading

PRAISE

Jane's book I'm feeling inspired, grateful, optimistic and devoted to lead with my heart so that I can continue to nurture, support and empower those around me."
—Sophie Dodd, consultant, mother of two, dancer, and superhuman

"I enjoyed reading Jane Phipps's book, The Heart-Centered Leader. *Jane has poured her heart and soul into this book. Written with intelligence and humanity, it tells her personal and professional story: her life journey, migrating to Australia at the tender age of five from England, growing up, learning to be stoic in life and in work, and becoming a single mum who raised her daughter and studied and worked. I learnt a very important lesson from reading the book—that our social conditioning and childhood upbringing, in some circumstances, in abusive environments and family dynamics, as well as patriarchal cultures, has controlled us and has subjugated us, making us, especially women, put up with abusive and toxic workplaces and bosses. Yet, it's the people who showed us kindness and care who have inspired us to be good people who do good work. I wish I had access to such a book before embarking on a work career, and in certain cases, becoming a victim of toxic bosses and work environments that are not truly values based and led. Jane shows us that there is another way, a way of leading and working that does not stem from command-and-control cultures, that is inspired by heart and humanity. I recommend anybody who works and aspires to leadership, or is privileged to already be in a leadership role, to read and take stock and reevaluate their service inspired by the principles Jane sets out as a heart-based leader. As the Dalai Lama tells us, 'Kindness is my religion,' and kindness is free. We need kind leaders in our work and our world."*
—Anastasia Panayiotidis, consultant psychologist, coach, clinical family therapist, and community leader

Published in Australia by
Pages Road Media
Email: janephippsauthor@gmail.com

First published in Australia 2025
Copyright © Jane Phipps 2025

All rights reserved. No part of this publication may be reproduced, stored in a retrieval system, or transmitted, in any form or by any means without the prior written permission of the publisher, nor be otherwise circulated in any form of binding or cover other than that in which it is published and without a similar condition being imposed on the subsequent purchaser.

National Library of Australia Cataloguing in Publication entry

A catalogue record for this book is available from the National Library of Australia

ISBN 978-1-7640356-0-6 (paperback)
ISBN 978-1-7640356-1-3 (epub)

Edited for US publication by Cortni L. Merritt at SRD Editing Services
Cover design by Sam Art Studio
Layout by Sophie White Design

Printed by Ingram Spark

Selection from *Angel Meadow: Victorian Britain's Most Savage Slum* by Dean Kirby is reproduced with kind permission.

Disclaimer: All care has been taken in the preparation of the information herein, but no responsibility can be accepted by the publisher or author for any damages resulting from the misinterpretation of this work. All contact details given in this book were current at the time of publication, but are subject to change.

The advice given in this book is based on the experience of the individuals. Professionals should be consulted for individual problems. The author and publisher shall not be responsible for any person with regard to any loss or damage caused directly or indirectly by the information in this book.

The Heart-Centered Leader

*Transformation and Healing
from Narcissistic Abuse
to Self-Empowerment*

JANE PHIPPS

DEDICATION

I would like to dedicate this book to my daughter, Lydia. It's been me and you side by side, facing whatever life throws our way. We've weathered storms together, leaned on each other for strength, and through it all, you have shown consistent resilience and grace. You are my inspiration and my greatest blessing.

*Figure 1:
Lydia at 3 months old*

About the Author

Jane Phipps is a transformational leader, consultant, and executive with more than two decades of experience navigating—and reshaping—complex workplaces across education, not-for-profit, and government sectors. With a background in mathematics and a career forged in some of the most challenging workplace environments, Jane has led million-dollar transformation projects, modernized operations, and built high-performing, values-driven teams.

As a former chief operating officer, Jane gained recognition for her strategic leadership, people-first mindset, and bold advocacy for inclusive and psychologically safe workplaces. She was a finalist for the 2024 Outstanding Leadership Award in Executive Leadership and a certified Mental Health First Aider.

Jane's leadership journey hasn't always been easy. As a single mum, a woman in male-dominated industries, and a survivor of workplace bullying and narcissistic abuse, she brings a deeply personal lens to leadership. Her approach is heart-centered—grounded in emotional intelligence, resilience, and integrity. She believes great leadership starts from within.

Jane is a sought-after advisor who champions emerging leaders and helps organizations align their strategies with their people. She currently runs her own consultancy and continues to mentor rising professionals through career and life transitions.

She lives in Melbourne with her demanding fur-boss Duchess the cat and is known for her dry wit, fierce loyalty, and unapologetic belief in human-first philosophy in all things.

Contents

About the Author 11
Foreword by Fiona Wainrit 15
Disclaimer 17
Introduction 19
Who Is This Book For? 21
My Journey 22

Part 1. The Leadership Wake-Up Call 29

Command-and-Control Leadership: A Relic from the Past 30
Diversity and Inclusion: Beyond the Buzzwords 45
Margarita's Story: A Journey Through Adversity and Transformation 50

Part 2. The Blueprint for Jane's Approach to Leadership 59

Heart-Centered Leadership: From Concept to Reality 60
The Core Five 66
A Tale of Two CEOs 73
Lavinia's Story: A Journey on her Own Terms 81

Part 3. The Hidden Ingredients of Great Leadership 85

Psychological Safety: The Secret Sauce 86
Emotional Intelligence: The Nonnegotiable 101
Josh's Story: A Journey Through Redefining Purpose 109
Mary's Story: A Journey with Technical Hurdles 114

Part 4. The Moments That Make a Difference — 119

The Leadership Confidence Trap — 120

My Defining Moment: Leaving Trauma and Toxicity Behind — 127

Eve's Story: A Geek's Journey to Leadership — 140

Part 5. My Inner Transformation — 149

From Survival Mode to Heart Mode: My Self-Empowerment — 150

Jon's Story: A Journey to Leadership Coaching — 164

Part 6. A Practical Guide to Leading with Heart — 169

How to Lead with Heart — 170

Lead Self — 175

Lead Others — 178

Lead Culture — 181

Part 7. Where is Leadership Headed? — 185

Looking Back: A Journey Through Leadership and Growth — 186

Gratitude — 196

References — 198

Glossary of Terms — 203

Would You Like to Work with Jane? — 209

Foreword by Fiona Wainrit

I feel deeply proud writing this foreword to *The Heart-Centered Leader*—not only as a career coach, but as someone who's lived many of the truths in these pages. At a recent catch-up, I half-joked (but fully meant it) that Jane should write a book. She had a story—many stories, actually—that needed to be heard. We'd often found ourselves in deep conversations about leadership—me from my coaching perspective, and Jane from her executive experience—particularly about workplace dynamics, narcissistic leaders, bullying, dysfunctional teams, and the unseen toll of toxic cultures. It was clear her perspective, lived experience, and hard-won insights had the power to shift the leadership conversation entirely. And now, here it is.

This is not your standard leadership book. It's not stuffed with academic theory or one-size-fits-all frameworks. It's raw, real, and refreshingly human. You'll find yourself highlighting entire paragraphs, nodding along, and maybe even tearing up—because Jane doesn't hold back. She shares her story with fierce vulnerability, and in doing so, gives voice to what so many experience but rarely say out loud. Jane's heart-centered leadership model challenges the traditional, power-based approach to leadership. Through compelling stories of diverse leaders, she demonstrates how empathy, genuineness, and a people-first approach create not merely healthier workplaces, but exceptional ones. The chapter on the Hidden Ingredients of Great Leadership [chapter 3] particularly resonated with me—revealing how psychological safety forms the foundation upon which all other leadership qualities can flourish.

As a solo mum by choice, I share with Jane the unique journey of raising children on our own and having worked in male-dominated industries and supported hundreds of clients through workplace trauma. I can say this with confidence: this book is the antidote to performative leadership. It's for anyone who's ever been silenced, sidelined, gaslit, or told they're "too sensitive" when they speak up. Jane shows us that psychological safety isn't a nice-to-have—it's the cornerstone of great leadership. Through deeply personal stories and practical strategies, she lays out a model of leadership grounded in courage, self-reflection, and emotional intelligence. Despite decades of executive experience across many sectors, Jane writes with humility and heart. She's someone who walks her talk, and it shows. Her leadership has not only created inclusive, psychologically safe workplaces, but also earned her recognition as a finalist for the 2024 Outstanding Executive Leadership Award. That speaks volumes. She doesn't pretend to have all the answers—and that's what makes her message even more powerful. What she does offer is wisdom earned through adversity, a people-first philosophy, and a timely reminder that strong leadership starts with self-awareness, kindness, and courage.

For anyone who's ever felt the sting of working under narcissistic or fear-based leadership, this book offers both validation and a way forward. It's a beacon for current and future leaders who are ready to ditch the ego, challenge toxic norms, and lead with compassion and clarity. Jane's words remind us that strength isn't about control—it's about heart. And in a world that desperately needs more human-centred leadership, this book couldn't be more timely.

Fiona Wainrit

Master Career Coach | Founder of Career Mojo

Disclaimer

This book is based on real experiences, both my own and those of others who have generously shared their stories. However, due to legal and ethical considerations, names, locations, and identifying details have been changed to protect the individuals involved.

While the lessons, themes, and challenges described here are entirely true and lived, any resemblance to specific people or organizations is coincidental. The purpose of this book is not to expose individuals, but rather to shed light on toxic leadership, workplace bullying, and the power of heart-centered leadership as a transformative approach.

This book does not provide legal or psychological advice. If you are experiencing workplace bullying, narcissistic abuse, or any form of harassment, I encourage you to seek professional support and guidance.

Introduction

Leadership is about people, not power. Yet too commonly, leadership is framed as a hierarchical system built on control and fear. This book challenges that notion by introducing a bespoke heart-centered leadership model that prioritizes empathy, genuineness, and a people-first approach.

Through my own lived experiences—navigating male-dominated industries, enduring toxic workplaces, and overcoming the psychological scars of parental narcissistic abuse, I have forged a leadership philosophy grounded in resilience that delivers high-performing empowered successful teams.

This book combines raw personal stories, real-life leadership challenges, and practical guidance to help you build your own heart-centered leadership approach that is effective but also ethical and fulfilling. Each chapter takes you on a roller coaster journey through challenges, learning, and personal anecdotes, providing real stories, key insights, and practical strategies.

Chapter 1: The Leadership Wake-Up Call sets the foundations for why leadership needs to change, by exploring my ancestral background and my journey from birth into the workplace. It ends with Margarita's story of navigating toxic workplaces and finding her strength to challenge harmful leadership.

Chapter 2: The Blueprint for Jane's Approach to Leadership explores the core principles of my bespoke heart-centered leadership model, explaining what it means to lead with genuineness, trust, respect, transparency, and vulnerability. It explores the guiding principles of service and support and introduces necessary environmental conditions. Lavinia's journey ends this chapter, with confidence and self-belief being used to define her own terms.

Chapter 3: The Hidden Ingredients of Great Leadership builds on the leadership model, exploring the often-overlooked soft skills that help define a workplace culture and a heart-centered leader: psychological safety and emotional intelligence. We conclude this chapter with Josh's experiences of controlling and heartfelt leadership and Mary's story of overcoming systematic bias.

Chapter 4: The Moments That Make a Difference is the most difficult chapter for me, deeply personal and emotional. This is where I demonstrate vulnerability and share the defining moments of my narcissistic upbringing being reflected in toxic workplaces, how it took me down, and how I dug deep to bring myself back up. Eve shares a similar experience: how her upbringing brought her to a place where she loves to geek-out on leadership theories.

Chapter 5: My Inner Transformation is the *so what?* chapter. True leadership starts from within. So, what did I learn from those defining moments? What did I learn by finally breaking free from the repeated patterns of my life? Read this chapter to find out. This chapter closes with a final story of how Jon's personal development and self-reflection transformed his ability to coach leadership.

Chapter 6: A Practical Guide to Leading with Heart is where you get to take over. This is where theory meets action. In this chapter, you'll find tangible, actionable steps to guide your work toward defining your own heart-centered style. Following soon from this book will be a goal-setting and reflective practice workbook, *The Heart-Centered Leader Workbook*.

Chapter 7: Where Is Leadership Headed brings all the pieces together and leaves you with something to think about; why are we still blaming the people who are bullied for the way they are treated? How does leading from the heart create a ripple effect for change?

INTRODUCTION

Who Is This Book For?

Are you an emerging leader? If you are stepping into leadership or management for the first time, this book will guide you, one step at a time, to develop a people-centric approach that is genuine, courageous, and human.

Are you already a leader seeking to grow? Whether in your workplace or your community, if you want to shift from traditional, hierarchical leadership to an uplifting, human-centered style, this book will give you thoughts to challenge in your current practice and changes to mull over.

Are you experiencing poor leadership? If you're currently working under a toxic or ineffective leader, this book can help you understand what's really happening. Whether it helps you take action, set boundaries, or seek change, it's here to empower you.

Are you a survivor of toxic leadership or a toxic workplace? If you've been bullied, manipulated, or gaslighted in the workplace, this book will validate your experiences and help you move forward with strength. You are not alone.

Are you recovering from narcissistic abuse? Whether from a parent, a boss, or a partner, narcissistic abuse leaves deep scars that are long lasting. This book offers insight into other people's experiences and shows you how common it is.

This book is here to remind you that your heart is your greatest leadership strength.

Your journey starts here. Are you ready?

My Journey

Leadership isn't about a fancy title, a corner office, or how many people report to you. It's not about power. It's about people. It's about creating an environment where they can thrive. It's about trust, and it's about impact. I didn't learn this from a textbook or a leadership seminar. It came from the messy, chaotic, real-life experiences of navigating my career as a single mum, a woman in male-dominated industries, and someone who's had to fight to be heard.

I grew up in a working-class family where grit and determination were part of our daily life, part of our DNA. My mum and dad, born in the working-class north of England, made a bold decision to leave everything behind and move to Tasmania, Australia, when I was a young five years old. They wanted more for me and my brother than what they had growing up in the birthplace of the Industrial Revolution. It was a life-changing move, and in many ways, it shaped the resilience and adaptability that I would later rely on throughout my life and career. There was no escaping that my family's DNA was deeply rooted in hierarchy and authority; as patriarchal tradition dictated, my dad was the breadwinner, my mum the homemaker. The rules were clear. The belief that "those in charge always know best" was ingrained in me from a young age. As I traveled along my personal, career, and leadership journeys, however, I came to challenge that narrative. I knew deep down that leadership wasn't about power—it was about people.

INTRODUCTION

Where Did It Start?

My first major job after university landed me in a heavily male-dominated Australian defense project. I was in my late twenties, one of the few women in a mathematical-based field, juggling my ambition with the responsibilities of being a single parent to a daughter in primary school (yes, I was an early starter). It wasn't easy. I faced discrimination and exclusion at every turn. One day, I wasn't competent enough. The next, I was *too* competent and "showing up the men." I was paid less. I was given less credit. The frustration in the office was *palpable* every time I had to leave *on time* to pick up my daughter from after-school care.

Despite it all, I loved my job. I was good at it. Most importantly, I loved my daughter, and I refused to let either responsibility slip. Then, in the middle of the chaos, I met a leader who would change my perspective forever and shape my leadership journey.

The leader in question was an American ex-military man—firm, decisive, but kind and clear in his direction. He was regularly seen walking the floor, chatting with people, not checking up on them or discussing work.

"How are the girls, Jane?" he would ask, knowing that I doted on my cats.

I admired him greatly, but there came a defining moment when my respect grew exponentially. It came on a particularly tough day when the male-dominated undermining reached boiling point. I was told to "pull my head in" by a particularly misogynistic colleague after standing up to him about his actions negatively impacting people and their work. I'd had enough. I marched straight into the CEO's office, past his executive assistant (who tried to stop me until she saw the look on my face), and told him exactly what was happening.

"I've had enough! We are all working hard to bring this project home, and this undermining bullshit is not helping."

Normally, in that kind of environment, my behavior would have been career suicide, but he stopped what he was doing, looked at me, and listened. He let me vent and then he acted. He organized a meeting of all parties, listened to all sides and then took action by reassigning the misogynist.

Later he told me, "If you were upset enough to behave so unusually and come straight to me, I knew it had to be important. I value your opinion and your courage."

That was it. That was the moment I understood leadership. It wasn't about titles or hierarchy. It wasn't about who had the loudest voice in the room. It was about who had the courage to speak up, and who had the integrity to listen. That moment helped shape the leader I wanted to be—someone who could balance technical ability with empathy, intelligence with kindness, strategy with respect. We live in a time of change with a profound shift in leadership. The old-school command-and-control approach—the one that ruled the corporate world for decades—is crumbling.

Millennials and Gen Z aren't buying into it anymore; they are stepping into the professional world with new expectations. They don't want to work for fear-based, hierarchical organizations where authority is worshipped and psychological safety is nonexistent. They expect their leaders to be purpose-driven, to be willing to listen and to empower. This isn't a passing trend. It's a full-scale transformation, and it's forcing current leaders to shake off the shackles and rethink what leadership actually means.

This book is my answer to that call.

It's a blend of personal journey and professional lessons—a mix of stories, experiences, and practical strategies. Some of them are hard-earned lessons from my own struggles, and some come from the incredible teams I've had the privilege to lead. I'll introduce my bespoke heart-centered leadership model and its philosophy grounded in principles that create workplaces where people feel safe to innovate, grow, and succeed. This isn't simply another leadership book. It's part memoir, part guidebook, and part call to action. I hope that as you read, you see pieces of your own story in mine.

I don't have all the answers. I'm not a leadership guru, nor a psychologist, nor do I believe in one-size-fits-all leadership. What I can offer are insights from my lived experience, practical strategies, and a different way of thinking about leadership. My hope is that this book will resonate with leaders at all stages of their journey, from those recently starting out to seasoned professionals seeking a fresh perspective, I would be honored to play a role in your leadership journey by passing on my lessons.

As you read, I invite you to reflect on:

- What kind of leader do you want to be?
- How can you create environments where trust and respect flourish?
- How can you use your past to shape your future?
- How can you lead in a way that drives results but also leaves a legacy?

At the end of the day, leadership isn't about being perfect. It's about being human. It's about being willing to grow. In a world crying out for connection, leading with the heart isn't merely a choice—it's the future.

So, let's begin.

Figure 2:
The house my family lived in when we moved to Tasmania, Australia, in 1971

INTRODUCTION

> "Each time a woman stands up for herself, without knowing it possibly, without claiming it, she stands up for all women."

—Maya Angelou, American memoirist, poet, and civil rights activist

> "What does not kill me makes me stronger."

—Friedrich Nietzsche, German philosopher, poet, and scholar

1

The Leadership Wake-Up Call

Command-and-Control Leadership: A Relic from the Past

First, a note: You'll notice that I use the word *leader* a lot. Occasionally, I'll swap it out for *manager* or *boss* depending on the context. However, because someone holds the title doesn't mean they are a true leader. As you read, you'll see exactly what I mean.

> **Definition: Command-and-control leadership** is a traditional top-down approach to management that involves a leader making decisions and giving orders to employees.

In the introduction, I mentioned a CEO who had a profound impact on me—someone who shaped my vision for leadership in ways I couldn't fully appreciate at the time. I also mentioned my North England roots, and before I fully understood what good leadership looked like, I had already spent years witnessing what it shouldn't be.

My dad's approach to parenting mirrored the command-and-control leadership style he had experienced throughout his own life. It was a model built on authority, discipline, and control, one that both challenged and shaped me, as a child, a leader, a mother, and a human being. The parallels between narcissistic parenting and authoritarian leadership were ingrained in my early experiences, and those experiences followed me into the workplace, where I encountered the same patterns of bullying, misogyny, and toxic control.

> **Definition: Bullying** is seeking to harm, intimidate, or coerce (someone perceived as vulnerable).

As a child trying to navigate my dad's expectations, and later as a woman in male-dominated workplaces, I felt conflicted when power was wielded in similar ways. Through that conflict, I also found clarity. The stark contrast between my dad's leadership and the examples set by others—like my granddad and later, the kind CEO—became the foundation for the leader I chose to become.

To understand where my journey began, let me give you some context by sharing a bit about my family. It will show you the birth of my evolution toward heart-centered leadership and away from narcissistic parenting and command-and-control leadership.

My dad was born in the outskirts of Manchester, in the North of England, at the end of World War II, the youngest of four. Before my dad had his first birthday, his dad was killed in a workplace accident on the Manchester docks, leaving my nanna alone to raise a baby, a ten-year-old, and two teenagers in a time of extreme poverty. I've heard stories about my dad as a child—wild, rebellious, always in trouble; he skipped school so much that he barely learned to read and write, causing endless difficulties for my nanna. So much so, when his oldest sister got married, the newlyweds inherited her youngest brother as their surrogate child. Even then, structure and discipline were scarce. His education remained minimal, and he turned to petty theft. Eventually, he started an apprenticeship as a carpet layer, where at sixteen, he met my mum, who was only fifteen and working in the office. My mum's story was equally shaped by hardship. The youngest of four, she lost her mum when she was only four years old. My granddad, an ex–coal miner forced into early retirement due to mining-related health issues, suddenly had to raise four children alone, struggling to provide for them.

By the time Mum and Dad married at eighteen and nineteen, they were a young couple, like many others, trying to build a life in the industrial north. My dad worked in a paper mill, my mum in a factory sewing police uniforms—a sweatshop by today's standards.

Then at nineteen, my mum had me. Three years later, my brother Christopher arrived. Our family story is not unique. It is a working-class reality shared by countless others—parents doing their best, surviving on what little they had.

However, survival came at a cost.

My dad was a narcissist—there, I've said it. Whether that trait was born or bred is a debate I won't get into; my intention here is to tell my story and how it shaped my life and leadership style. What I know is this: his parenting style was authoritarian, critical, and controlling.

> **Definition: Narcissism** is a personality trait or disorder that involves an exaggerated sense of self-importance, a lack of empathy, and a need for admiration.

Encouragement was conditional. Praise was given only when it aligned with his ego and expectations. When it didn't align, there was punishment—sometimes in words, sometimes in silence, sometimes in an unpredictable explosion of rage. Years later, I saw how his approach routinely paralleled the behaviors of command-and-control leaders in the workplace, where those who lacked sufficient experience or knowledge resorted to control when relying on subordinates' expertise to get things done.

I digress slightly, by bringing you into one of my passions, but don't worry, there is a link to my story. I am obsessed with ancestry, and my research has taken me to explore a significant historical region of Manchester called Angel Meadows, where ancestors from both sides of my family lived. Was it living? This place has been described as the vilest and most dangerous slum of the Industrial Revolution by Dean Kirby in his book *Angel Meadow: Victorian Britain's Most Savage Slum*. The following paragraph from his book (reproduced with kind permission) will give you some insight of the horrendous conditions that my English and Irish ancestors battled a little over a century ago. It gave me great insight into the impact of command-and-control mindset and behaviors.

Life was tough in the mills around Angel Meadow. Some of these great black buildings employed up to 2000 hands in vast industrial colonies, where the working day was governed by the rise and fall of steam engines. Children risked death and serious injury to scavenge pieces of cotton beneath the fast-moving machines. The working day at 5 a.m., with a piece of bread and a cup of weal tea for breakfast, usually without milk. Porridge was rarely eaten in the slum.

Before dawn, the streets thronged with men, women and children heading to work. Some queued for coffee or cocoa sold by street vendors. The factory bells began to ring for five minutes before 6 a.m. Then the engines roared into life perfectly on time. The mill hands worked in silence amid the chattering machinery. Anyone who was late would find the doors locked and lose half a day's wages.

At 1 p.m., the engines fell silent, and the workers stopped for dinner. Crowds of hungry people swarmed into the streets, and lanes that had been silent minutes earlier now echoed with hundreds of clogs. The workers went home and ate a few boiled potatoes or scraps of bacon fried with lard. Some visited cook shops for a meat and potato pie. After dinner, they had just enough time to smoke a pipe before the factory bells ordered them back to work.

Now that you have a mental picture of my ancestors' working conditions, let us return to the story. As a child, I had two competing influences—my dad's rigid control and my granddad's quiet guidance, which had a strong and lasting influence. My granddad followed us to Australia a year after we emigrated, and for six years, he was my lifeline. Upon reflection, he was the first true leader in my life: kind, patient, and wise, and he was my first example of *balancing head and heart*. He didn't demand obedience; he taught me through kindness and examples.

We played draughts (checkers) for hours, but he never let me win. Instead, he taught me his tactics and his thinking until I could beat him fairly. That, I now realize, was empowerment. He believed in my intelligence and nurtured it. By the time I started school he had already taught me basic reading, writing, and math. That was lovely, and mum and granddad were very proud of me; however, it made me an easy target for bullying, particularly from my cousin, who hadn't received the same attention from our granddad. Her continued bullying through my school life served to constantly remind me of her jealousy.

Like me, my mum also learned kindness from my granddad and used it along with her affection for me and my brother to soften my dad's approach. This early experience with bullying and favoritism, along with my mum's support started to shape my resilience early, but it also started to give me a glimpse of how power dynamics work. It was a lesson that later I would see repeated in the workplace—where leaders reward those who stroke their egos and punish those who threaten them. The encouragement from my mum and granddad sparked my lifelong interest to learn and to question, understand, and grow.

My dad, however? He didn't see my intelligence as an asset. He saw it as defiance. My dad was the epitome of command-and-control leadership. In his world, he was always right; his authority was absolute. Questions were met with hostility, mistakes with shame, and independence with resistance. I can hear his voice:

"Don't answer back."
"Don't question me."
"Do as you're told."

My curiosity was treated as insubordination. It mirrored the way weak leaders in the workplace react when their authority is questioned. Like many command-and-control leaders, my dad didn't handle highly skilled or independent people well. He valued control over growth. He dismissed my academic achievements (or credited himself for them) but criticized me relentlessly when I struggled with sports, something he valued. Unfortunately, Christopher's lack of sportiness was criticized even more so—because he was a *boy*!

This introduces the paradox of toxic leadership—when their people succeed in ways they don't understand, they feel threatened instead of proud.

Talented employees resist micromanagement. They push back when their expertise is ignored. The more command-and-control leaders tighten their grip, the more independent thinkers slip through their fingers. My dad's narrow focus left me feeling unworthy. The absolute power of a commanding leader or parent can create toxicity. For me, the effects of experiencing an autocratic parent mirrored those of working under similar leadership in the workplace. Both dynamics are ego-driven and leave little room for empathy, growth, or mutual respect.

In contrast, my mum's ability to see *the best in people* along with my granddad's influence remain foundational to my personal values and leadership philosophy. They both lived a life of integrity and resilience: they taught me about being a decent human being and balancing intelligence with compassion. They both found strength through their struggles. These lessons laid the foundation for my belief in modern heart-centered leadership and continue to inspire my advocacy for this approach in today's workplaces. Does my dad deserve blame for his style of parenting, or did it come from an era when that was the way of the world? I don't know if I will ever have that answer.

> **Statistics:** According to PsychiatryUK, studies show that bullying is a growing issue that has a negative impact on people's careers, lives, and well-being. 47% of UK workers have observed bullying at work—while one in ten have actually experienced being bullied in the workplace.

"Workplace bullying—in any form—is bad for business. It destroys teamwork, commitment, and morale."

—Tony Morgan, former chief executive, The Industrial Society

"More and more, when I single out the person who inspired me most, I go back to my grandfather."

—James Earl Jones, American award-winning screen and Broadway actor, father

Figure 3:
My mum in 1965, outside my nanna's house
in Radcliffe, England

> "If you give an education to a girl, that's how you're changing her life and that's how you're also changing the world."

—Malala Yousafzai, Nobel laureate, author and speaker, education activist

Figure 4: Me and my dad on our holidays in 1967

Do What I Say!

Our workplaces are continually evolving, and it's become increasingly clear that the approach from the past no longer serves modern organizations or the people within them. Command-and-control leadership relies heavily on hierarchy, with decisions flowing down from the top. Leaders of this ilk frequently exert their authority to drive results, using fear or strict discipline to maintain control. While this might have worked in factories or military settings of the past, it's a poor fit for the knowledge-based, collaborative workplaces of today.

I have a recent example of this. One executive I worked with made it painfully clear how deeply embedded this mindset still is even though we may think it is long gone. During a meeting, she turned to her team and, with absolute sincerity, said:

"I am an executive, and you need to do what I say."

The room fell uncomfortably silent. The team she was addressing were experts in their fields, dedicated professionals who knew the specifics of their work better than she did. Instead of collaboration and striving for the best outcome, she demanded unwavering obedience. When they asked for some context and clarity on what she wanted—she labeled them "change resistant." Behind closed doors, she went even further, openly admitting she planned to push them out—to make their lives uncomfortable until they left, allowing her to replace them with people who wouldn't question her authority. I wondered why a leader would think like this and why she would share her outdated beliefs with her executive peers. I finally concluded she was working from a place of fear because she was dealing with a team of subject matter experts who were technically outstanding, and their need to seek context was seen as a challenge to her authority.

It was my dad all over again.

Modern teams don't need dictators. They need leaders who listen, who empower, and who build environments where people can be themselves. This executive had an opportunity for shared success right in front of her. If she had taken a moment to provide the *why*—the context behind her vision—the team could have brought their expertise to the table and figured out the *how*. By choosing positional power over conversation, she shut down a multitude of possibility.

I like to think that the world has changed or is in the throes of changing. Leadership needs to change with it. AI is here, and it is going to free up time for humans to be humans rather than cogs in an industrial wheel.

Later in this book, I will share my defining moment, when working for a narcissistic, command-and-control leader became a life-changing experience—one that helped me heal from past wounds and reaffirm my commitment to leading and living from my heart.

We don't have to lead the way we were led.

We get to choose a different path, our own path.

Statistics: According to the Recovery Village, approximately 1 in 200 people of the United States population has **Narcissistic Personality Disorder**, about 75% of those are men. About 15% of people with this disorder also have depression, 13.5% have anxiety, and 17.5% have another mood disorder.

The Crumbling Facade

The cracks in the foundations of command-and-control leadership have been visible for years. High turnover rates, disengaged employees, and stagnant innovation are a few of the warning signs that it simply isn't working anymore.

I have felt this firsthand. There were times in my career when I became unmotivated—not because I wasn't passionate about my work, but because I was stuck in an environment where I couldn't ask for clarification. I remember being asked to rework the same tasks again and again, only to land right back where we started. It was frustrating beyond belief, and I know I'm not alone in this—if you're nodding along, sighing in agreement, you've been there too. That feeling of being unmotivated is something internal, something with which we wrestle within ourselves. Demotivation? That's different. That results from external factors—suffocation, micromanagement, fear of speaking up. When people feel like mere cogs in a machine, their productivity drops, their passion fades, and their willingness to go above and beyond disappears. In industries that thrive on creativity and innovation, command-and-control leadership doesn't nurture potential—it kills it.

By contrast, when I stepped into a leadership role with a team that had previously been under a strict command-and-control leader, I saw the impact of that conditioning. The team was hesitant, constantly seeking permission before making even the smallest decisions. They had been trained to avoid mistakes and to play it safe. The interactions between the team members were uncomfortable for me to see, they were stifled. It took time to rebuild, to show them that they were safe to speak up, to contribute, and to take ownership of their work. I made a conscious effort to create an open and collaborative environment—celebrating small wins, actively listening, and encouraging initiative. Slowly, things changed. The team's confidence grew. They took ownership and came up with innovative ideas.

The difference between my approach and the dictatorial "do as I say" stood out. The controlled team was toxic with a staff turnover rate of almost 50 percent, and a higher-than-average number of employees seeking support from the Employee Assistance Program. Meanwhile, my team thrived. Not because I was a perfect leader, but because of the value I placed on my people.

The Real Price of Leading Through Fear

Margot Faraci's *Love Leadership Survey* highlights a brutal truth—fear-based leadership doesn't simply make workplaces unpleasant; it makes them unworkable. Leaders who rely on fear create discomfort actively pushing people away, leaving behind anxious, hesitant employees who are more focused on self-preservation than on innovation. They are in survival mode. Joshua M. Evans takes this one step further, pointing out that fear-based leadership is one of the fastest ways to lose top talent. In today's job market, talented individuals have options. They don't need to stay in toxic environments where they feel undervalued or disrespected. When they do leave, the ripple effect is devastating—key skills walk out the door, client relationships suffer, and the remaining employees are left demoralized, wondering if they should be the next to go. If an organization is in the middle of growth or transformation, that kind of talent drain can be catastrophic.

This is not simply theory—the numbers back it up.

Gallup's research shows that companies with higher levels of engaged employees and talented managers earn 147 percent higher earnings per share than those that don't. The message is crystal clear: workplaces that engage, support, and empower their people perform better than those that rule through fear. Margot Faraci's research reinforces this—leaders who rely on fear create disengaged teams, and disengaged teams fail. The organizations that succeed are the ones that create environments where people feel safe, valued, and free to bring their full selves to work.

That is where psychological safety comes in.

Harvard Business School Professor Amy Edmondson, who introduced the term *psychological safety*, defines it as a shared belief that an environment is safe for interpersonal risk-taking. In simple terms—it means people can ask questions, share concerns, admit mistakes, and experiment without fear of humiliation or punishment. Fear-based leadership keeps people stuck. Psychological safety moves them forward. For me, psychological safety is more than a theory—it's personal, and it's a passion.

Years ago, I worked under a dictator (and that's not only my opinion—it was widely shared by his entire team and others). His presence was suffocating, and his leadership style marred by control, intimidation, and punishment. His team members were miserable, constantly on edge, wondering what his next move would be. It wasn't until he took a month's holiday, leaving me in charge that I realized how much damage he had done—not only to the team but to me personally. When he finally walked back into the office, something physical happened to me. My hands started trembling. My stomach flipped. Fear and nausea gripped me. I knew I was about to be punished. Not because I had failed to act on his behalf—but because I had succeeded in his absence.

It was another one of those defining moments—the kind that will surface frequently throughout this book. The moment when I knew, deep in my bones, that no job was worth feeling like this. It was a lesson I *should* have learned the first time it happened. Unfortunately, I didn't. That's one of the traits of fear-based leadership—it conditions you to normalize the fear until one day, your body refuses to play along anymore. Command-and-control leadership is crumbling for this reason—because people won't tolerate it anymore.

The workforce is changing. People want leaders who support them, not punish them. They want workplaces where they can speak up, not shrink back. They want psychological safety, not fear.

They want leaders who lead with heart.

> ## "Diversity is the mix. Inclusion is making the mix work."
>
> —Andrés Tapia, president of Diversity Best Practices

> ## "Diversity and Inclusion is a competitive advantage that a smart leader would not overlook."
>
> — Brian Ka Chan, AI expert, author and consultant, human rights activist

Diversity and Inclusion: Beyond the Buzzwords

A team is only as psychologically safe as its least safe member. That's a key takeaway from the article "Psychological Safety, Diversity & Inclusion" by Tom Geraghty. Often, those who feel the least safe in an organization are individuals who are already marginalized, underrepresented, or disadvantaged.

> **Definition: Lived experience** refers to an individual's personal and subjective encounters, including emotions, perceptions, and knowledge gained through direct, firsthand involvement in everyday events.

If we ignore people's lived experiences, identities, pronouns, past traumas, or the systemic inequalities they face, we risk creating a false environment, one that only benefits those already privileged enough to not worry about such challenges. True psychological safety doesn't mean that a handful of people feel safe to speak up, it means everyone feels safe to speak up.

The playing field isn't level yet. Addressing inequities in the workplace is a moral responsibility and a necessity if organizations want to unlock the full benefits of psychological safety. If people don't feel seen, valued, and heard, then they don't feel safe.

I remember one of my team members, a very well-educated Indian female engineer in a male-dominated environment. She was kind, intelligent, and hardworking, but instead of feeling comfortable asserting herself, she leaned into her cultural background to try to fit in. She started cooking food for the entire team every Friday, and at first, it seemed like a nice gesture—until I noticed my male counterparts casually placing "orders." I pulled her aside and gently asked her to consider what was happening. She admitted she had fallen into this role subconsciously—it was her way of attempting to gain acceptance.

We brainstormed together about what would feel comfortable for her. While she insisted on still cooking once a month because she genuinely enjoyed it, she also realized her value to the team wasn't in the food she brought but in the mathematical expertise and skills she contributed. I had a much harder conversation with those male managers. They needed to understand that their role was to guide younger team members, not take advantage of an unconscious gender dynamic. Slowly, the situation shifted, and she grew confident in asserting herself in the team as an equal. Truth be told we all enjoyed her monthly cooking sessions, and she started something because others eventually contributed their cooking talents.

This experience is a small but telling example of how inclusivity—or the lack of it—impacts culture. Today's workforce is far less tolerant of environments where people feel like outsiders. Today's employees, particularly Millennials and Gen Z, have completely different expectations from the generations before them. They aren't interested in old-school command-and-control leadership. They value collaboration, purpose, and inclusivity over hierarchy and obedience.

If they don't feel heard, they'll leave.

Younger employees are far keener on quitting jobs that don't align with their values. A great example is the rise of *naked resigning*—where people leave without having another job lined up because staying in a toxic environment feels worse than financial instability. I think about this in the context of single parents and families. Not everyone is in the right circumstances to make the ultimate move and quit. I certainly wasn't. When I was raising my daughter alone, I had to grit my teeth and push through at jobs that were far from ideal, simply because I couldn't risk losing financial security. Many people face this struggle, stuck in places where they don't feel valued.

That's exactly why leadership needs to change.

The best organizations are already adapting to these expectations by creating workplaces where people feel that they belong. It's not entirely about being a nice leader—it's also about staying relevant. Leaders who refuse to adapt—who cling to authority and refuse to listen—push away the very people who will shape the organization's future. For me, inclusive leadership wasn't something I learned in a management course. I learned it as a single mum raising my child, balancing ambition and survival, adapting constantly, and involving my daughter in everything. She sat with me while I did my university homework, came to lectures by my side, helped plan meals, organized the washing and ironing. I even included her in decisions around our budget. When we moved to another part of Australia—Melbourne, for my first post-university job—she understood the purpose behind the big life change because I included her in the *what, why,* and *how* of our journey.

I trusted her to contribute in ways she could, rather than dictating what she had to do. Of course I still had "because I said so" moments (I'm only human!), but at its core, our life was built on mutual respect and communication. Reflecting on this, I realize this is exactly what today's workforce wants from leadership. They want to be included. They want purpose. They want to contribute in meaningful ways.

I learned this organically through living my life, but I was hit hard when I stepped into the corporate world, right into the rigid walls of command-and-control leadership. It was a punch in the guts. I spent years navigating my dad's behavior and building a different life only to land in workplaces where dictatorship ruled the day. That was jarring, but it also reinforced what I already knew—I was going to continue to treat people better than how I was treated.

I didn't know then that it was heart-centered leadership.

When Leadership Fails to Listen

There's a concept called the Ostrich Effect, described in *Idea to Value*. It happens when leaders—and sometimes entire leadership teams—actively avoid bad news. Instead of confronting issues, they bury their heads in the sand, pretending everything is fine while the organization crumbles. It's no surprise that command-and-control environments breed this kind of delusion. When leaders rule through fear, employees stop telling the truth. Why risk their job by challenging leadership? Instead, they stay silent, nod along, and let bad decisions snowball into disasters.

A perfect example of this? The Australian Wheat Board. Once a trusted institution supporting Australian farmers, it became infamous for its role in the oil-for-food scandal. Internal warnings and concerns were dismissed or ignored, and the leadership closed ranks instead of listening. The result was a catastrophic collapse of trust, governance failure, and the eventual dismantling of the organization. It didn't fail because of poor workers—it failed because speaking up was punished, not protected. I've seen this exact pattern play out in my own career.

In one organization, leadership had an ambitious goal—to double the customer base within a year in an environment of financial instability. The problem? There was no investment in infrastructure to support that growth. No additional resources. No strategy to scale. I tried to flag this. I tried to propose a smarter plan—one that allowed for steady, sustainable expansion. Instead, I was vilified. I was shut down, labelled "resistant to change," and dismissed by executives who didn't want to hear reality. The result? They didn't hit their target. Customer engagement dropped, employee retention was worse than ever, and they ended in worse shape than when they started. The lesson? Heart-centered leadership is partially about being nice to people and providing a great culture, but it's also about making better business decisions. Companies succeed when they cultivate a culture of honest conversations and trust; companies fail when they silence people.

A success story can be found with Mondragon, a Spanish cooperative where employees are also owners. Everyone has a voice, and no decision is made without those voices being heard. When crisis hit during the global financial crisis, Mondragon didn't cut jobs, they shared the impact across the business. That's the kind of courageous, collective thinking that only happens when people feel safe to speak and empowered to lead.

Another example is Patagonia. Their employees are encouraged to speak up, challenge leadership, and act on their values and not only performance measures. Their culture of trust has created a profitable company and one with a legacy of environmental advocacy, ethical leadership, and loyalty that money can't buy.

These examples demonstrate organizations that encourage honest conversations, that empower people instead of silencing them, find success. Those that don't? They lose their edge, their talent, and eventually, their relevance.

Summarizing: The Command-and-Control Hangover

The old-school mindset that values hierarchy, rigidity, and fear-based management still hangs around in some organizations like an unwanted guest at a party. *Admired Leadership* call it the "command-and-control hangover," and if you've ever worked under a leader clinging to outdated power dynamics, you know exactly what I mean.

I get it—I've been pulled by this mindset myself. In my early leadership years, I occasionally caught myself leaning into control, especially under pressure. There were moments when, despite knowing better, the safety net of structure and authority lured me. I found myself exhausted and unfulfilled from micromanaging and fighting my values.

Breaking free from this hangover takes self-awareness and a willingness to get uncomfortable.

After Margarita's story, we will explore my bespoke heart-centered leadership model that I embraced while leaning into this discomfort.

Margarita's Story: A Journey Through Adversity and Transformation

Margarita's story is one of resilience, hard-fought lessons, and ultimately, self-reclamation. At thirty-two, she carries the weight of lived experiences that shaped her career and her understanding of leadership, power, and personal identity. Her journey—growing up in a turbulent household, finding refuge in education, navigating toxic workplaces, and discovering the impact of heart-centered leadership—offers a raw and compelling insight into the modern workplace and the kind of leadership we need for the future.

Margarita grew up in a military household, where structure and instability coexisted in uneasy tension. Her family moved frequently, spending time overseas, but home was never legitimately a safe place. "Mum and Dad both had big personalities. When they were good, they were good, but when they were bad, it was really bad," she recalls. "It always felt like me and my brother against the world."

Her brother, eighteen months older, became her protector—

buffering her from their mother's emotional volatility, particularly when their father was away on duty. Their mother lacked empathy and maternal warmth, while their father—once a source of security—became emotionally unstable after leaving the military. By the time Margarita was eight, her parents separated, and she and her brother chose to live with their father. "Before the split, Dad was our safe space—the one with empathy, the one who made us feel some semblance of love and security. But after the army, something changed in him." What followed was a chaotic adolescence. Her father cycled through relationships, her brother was eventually kicked out, and she found herself alone, dealing with the fallout of his emotional instability. Though he never physically hurt her, the violence around her left its mark.

Through it all, her grandma and granddad were her saving grace. "They were our safety net. I practically grew up in their house. My grandma was an incredible woman—strong, independent, born in the wrong time. She had a brilliant career as a nurse, but she gave it up to look after my granddad when he got sick."

Her most cherished memories are of running home from school to listen to Johnny Cash with her grandmother, eating a favorite after-school snack and listening to their song, "Daddy Sang Bass."

When her grandmother passed away, the last piece of her safety net disappeared. While home life was unpredictable, school became Margarita's lifeline. Teachers saw something in her that she hadn't yet seen in herself. "I could have gone down a bad path, but a teacher believed in me—believed I could be better if I only gave myself the chance. They got me involved in leadership activities, signed me up for programs over the holidays—anything to keep me busy and out of the house." That teacher changed her trajectory. She became school captain, the first in her family to go to university, and later, the first to pursue postgraduate studies.

"Education changed everything. It was my way out. The one

thing that was going to stop me from becoming my parents. I knew if I could get through university, I would never have to look back."

Breaking away came at a cost. No one in her family or circle of friends understood why she was constantly doing assignments, why she was pushing so hard. "It created a rift. No one around me had gone to university, so they didn't get it."

Still, she pressed on. She believed—*still* believes—that education is a world-changer, and that one day, she could use her lived experience to inspire others to break their own cycles.

Workplace Trauma: When History Repeats Itself

Despite the progress she made, the patterns of her childhood followed her into the workplace. So did the imposter syndrome.

"I looked like a cool, calm, and collected person on top, and everyone thought I was on top of everything, but underneath, I was a duck paddling with an ever-present belief that I had to do more, put more work in, work harder to prove that I deserved to be there."

In her last job, Margarita encountered a toxic manager who mirrored the same unpredictability and emotional manipulation she faced growing up. "I was love-bombed one moment, crucified the next. Praised in public, belittled in private. It was calculated. It was purposeful." Margarita had two challenges in this job, a personal one and a professional one that worked to feed each other. "I have done a lot of work on a personal level to fight self-doubt and imposter syndrome, to fight my childhood demons, and no way was someone going to make me believe I didn't belong." Margarita *had* done the self-work and knew she was good at her job. Still, Margarita's manager played into her self-doubt; she was able to bring it to the surface and activate Margarita's imposter syndrome. Margarita became a target of her boss, a narcisstic leader, one who thrived on control and fear, a true command-and-control leader that we have been discussing throughout this book.

"If I had been someone willing to roll over and say nothing, I probably wouldn't have been the focus of her wrath, but I wasn't. I challenged her. I started pulling the curtain back, telling the truth. That's when I became public enemy number one. The arrows weren't only for me anymore—my team became targets too. She knew I'd do anything to protect them." It was a war of attrition. The more Margarita stood up, the harder they came for her. "I felt like a person leaning over her team to protect them from the arrows in my back." Margarita's options were limited, her narcissist leader was protected by the CEO and by default empowered.

"I am a sensitive, empathic person, but I couldn't read my manager, I didn't know what version of her I was getting" Margarita's mind and body reacted with a trauma response, reminded of her childhood experiences. "I learnt that when I got home from school, I had to read what mood my dad was in. I had to determine if he had been drinking. I had to learn what version of my narcissistic mum I was getting by listening to the tone of her voice."

> **Definition: Burnout** is a state of emotional, physical, and mental exhaustion caused by excessive and prolonged stress.

Margarita did not feel safe in this workplace, which became apparent when her body started keeping score. She experienced chronic pain, health flare-ups, and the mental weight of burnout. She was constantly in fight-or-flight mode, reliving the same patterns from childhood—reading the room, assessing safety, waiting for the next emotional explosion. To make things worse, this workplace encouraged their people to share their personal story to build connections and align with the organization's purpose.

That vulnerability was turned against Margarita, her background was weaponized against her, the past used as a tool to undermine her sense of belonging. "Even my medical diagnosis, which I had shared in good faith, became another tool for discrimination. I had assumed I was in a safe space. I wasn't. I felt like I had walked straight into a trap."

Margarita stayed. She didn't believe she could do anything else. "I felt like the proverbial 'frog in boiling water.' I had normalized bad behavior. Not because I thought I deserved it, but because I had been conditioned to put up with it." Margarita felt alone and isolated; she lost her ability to trust, especially herself. Her safety net was gone. Luckily, she had some kind people around her. It took two kind but firm conversations from these people to bring her to her senses.

Her best friend told her, "I'd rather have you unemployed than dead.

A workplace colleague told her, "You are worth more than being treated like this."

She couldn't do it any longer. She left.

A Stark Contrast in Leadership Styles

Margarita knows firsthand the devastation that command-and-control leadership can inflict—professionally, physically, and emotionally. "Oh, I have been impacted badly by command-and-control leadership," she says. "Everything I've described—it took such a toll on me that I got physically and emotionally sick. I didn't know how to navigate it."

"Because of my background and always being off-kilter, I am the type of person that if you start pulling the walls in on me, I'm going to push further out. Especially when I see real injustice, when I see something is wrong, I'm not letting it lie." That's why she was drawn to work in an organization that was supposed to fight for the underdog—to make a difference for people who needed an advocate. "No matter what that narcissistic manager did, no matter how much damage she caused, one thing remains true: I still care how others around me are treated. That's never going to change. What has changed is that I've learned to not let it take as much hold."

She now understands that standing up for others doesn't mean sacrificing herself. Protecting people from toxic leadership is noble, but not at the expense of her own well-being.

The scars remain but so does her fire.

Margarita had known a different kind of leadership before the toxicity. Her first manager in the same organization had been everything her toxic boss wasn't—strong, compassionate, empowering. "She had high expectations, but she pushed me in the right way. She created a vision. She encouraged discussion and disagreement without fear. When I was grieving the loss of a close friend, she was the one who pulled me aside and said, "It's OK not to be OK. Let's get you some help." Margarita credits this manager for developing her own leadership philosophy of always expecting a team to do the right thing until there is evidence that they aren't, while setting clear boundaries.

Another leader in the organization—though not her direct manager—also left a profound impact. "She gave me the confidence and the permission to be fully myself. The first time I met her, I thought, I want to be like her when I'm older."

That was the contrast: One leader empowered, the other destroyed. One built trust, the other weaponized it. One made people feel safe, the other made them question themselves. Margarita has seen both ends of the leadership spectrum.

"I have learnt that heart-centered leaders will admit when they are wrong. They'll acknowledge when they don't know something, and they don't feel like they have to be the loudest voice in the room.

They have a willingness to learn. They hold themselves accountable. They don't pretend to know every detail of everyone's job—instead, they trust their team and listen to those who specialize." To Margarita, an undisputably strong leader doesn't need to dominate. They don't need absolute control to feel important. Instead, they create space for others to contribute, grow, and challenge ideas. "A heart-centered leader encourages discussion. They don't feel threatened by it. They actively look for ways to empower and develop the people they manage." In contrast, the command-and-control leader she worked under refused to allow dissent. "She would not let anyone disagree with her publicly, and if we did, we knew there would be consequences. She claimed to value open discussion, but in reality, she only wanted agreement. The moment you challenged her, you became a target."

Margarita believes controlling leaders avoid disagreement because they fear what it represents—growth, progress, and a shift in power dynamics. "That kind of leader comes in thinking they already know the right way to do everything. There's no willingness to learn, no interest in adapting. It's rigid, top-down leadership that discourages initiative and stifles innovation." She found the biggest difference between the two styles to be trust.

"Trust firstly. Then beyond that—empathy and self-awareness. Those were completely missing from the toxic leader I worked under. A command-and-control leader wants everyone to line up behind them. An empowering leader stands at the back, lifting people up."

Margarita believes that the future of leadership belongs to those willing to listen, learn, and lead with empathy. "The traits that matter? Willingness—to watch, listen, and grow. Trust—trusting people to do their jobs and make mistakes. Self-awareness—to admit when you're wrong. Humility—to know when you need to ask questions. Empathy—to understand the impact you have on the people around you." Most importantly, she believes that organizations need to stop criminalizing those who speak up. "No one speaks out about workplace bullying because the bully is protected, and the person who speaks up gets pushed out. That's what happened to me."

From Broken to Rebuilt: Margarita 2.0

Leaving that toxic workplace and having to return to her hometown without a job was devastating. She feared she had failed, had gone backward, but worst of all was the shame. "No one talks about the shame that comes with being bullied out of a job."

She rebuilt.
She set boundaries.
She learned what she would and wouldn't tolerate.
She realized her job was not her identity.

Now she sees toxic behavior quickly and calls it out. She no longer sacrifices herself for workplaces that don't deserve her.

"I am Margarita 2.0. I will never let myself be in that situation again."

> **Statistics:** American 2023 statistics: According to recent studies, a staggering 75% of employees have witnessed workplace bullying behavior (Seytan).

2

The Blueprint for Jane's Approach to Leadership

Heart-Centered Leadership: From Concept to Reality

Heart-centered leadership isn't merely a leadership style—it's a commitment. It's creating an environment where people feel valued, heard, and empowered to succeed. At its core, it's being a real human with an unwavering focus on what's best for people. The need to set priorities, workplans, and goals is all about management, and it goes without saying that this is necessary. Leadership is more than this: it's about people and how people successfully achieve goals. When leaders prioritize transparency, trust, respect, genuineness, and vulnerability, they build strong, resilient, and engaged teams. Successful teams.

That's why I developed, through my lived experience, my bespoke Heart-Centered Leadership model, to capture my leadership philosophy. The model consists of a framework that lives and breathes in an environment of psychological safety and emotional intelligence and is built on two essential pillars:

- **Support:** The structure that enables people to grow, experiment, and reach their potential.
- **Service:** The mindset that leadership is about uplifting, guiding, and empowering others.

Psychological safety and emotional intelligence are discussed at length in the next chapter, so let's start the exploration of the model by considering the essential pillars.

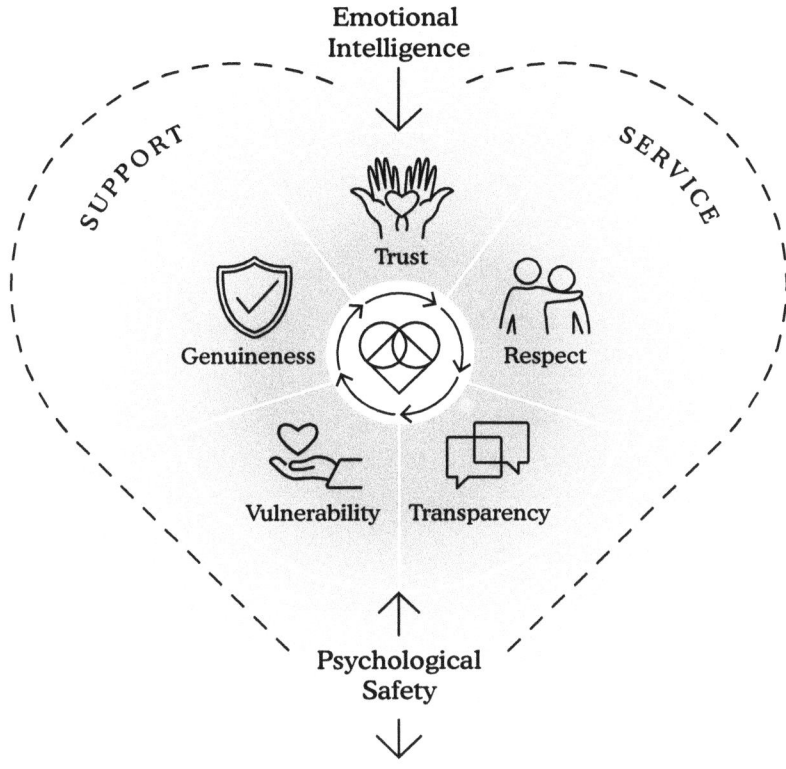

Figure 5: Jane's Heart-Centered Leadership Model

Leadership is about setting others up for success. Therefore, support cannot be limited to simple encouragement—it requires creating the conditions that allow people to thrive. That means giving them clarity, guidance, and resources so they can do their best work. What does true support look like?

- **Being present and accessible:** Great leaders show up. They're approachable, they listen, and they genuinely care.

- **Providing resources and frameworks:** Clear expectations, coaching, and tools give people confidence and assistance to succeed.

- **Removing obstacles:** Through advocacy, coaching, and direct action, they clear the path so their people can perform at their best.

- **Encouraging growth:** Investing in people's skills through mentorship, training, and feedback is one of the most important things a leader can do.

- **Creating a culture where asking for help is a strength:** In a supportive workplace, seeking guidance isn't a weakness—it's a sign of commitment to excellence.

On the flip side, command-and-control leaders fail in support by canceling important meetings, neglecting team needs, and providing little (if any) meaningful feedback. Some actively block progress by withholding information or failing to provide what's needed to move forward. This lack of support hinders performance, but it also erodes trust, damages morale, and creates a toxic work environment where people feel frustrated, undervalued, and disengaged. Heart-centered leaders do the opposite. They make sure support is invisibly woven into the team's culture, and no one succeeds alone.

Real leadership means standing beside your team, encouraging them, and giving them the necessary tools.

If support is the structure, then service is the mindset. Heart-centered leadership means serving the people you lead, helping them reach their goals, overcome challenges, and become the best version of themselves. Leaders who embrace service:

- **Put their people first:** They ask, "How can I help you succeed?" rather than "What can you do for me?"
- **Take responsibility for team well-being:** They create environments where people feel valued, appreciated, and secure.
- **Model integrity and accountability:** They "walk the talk."
- **Empower others to lead:** They lift up others, allowing them to shine and helping them grow into their own leadership style.

A leader who embodies service shifts the focus from power and control to empowerment and collaboration. This mindset inspires trust and respect, as people feel seen, heard, and supported. On the other hand, leaders who are self-serving, transactional, or power-driven create disengagement, resentment, and fear—the exact opposite of what a thriving workplace needs. Service is the heartbeat of my leadership style; when leaders serve their people, they cultivate environments where people are inspired to do their best work.

One of the first actions I take when I step into a new leadership role is to establish regular one-on-one meetings with each team member. These are a core part of how I lead, and I use them to create space for genuine connection, individual support, and developing trust. They help me understand how each person works best, what drives them, and what might be getting in their way. It's in these moments that the foundations of a high-performing team are built—one relationship at a time. And that is why I rarely cancel them.

If service and support are the two essential pillars, let's now look at what those pillars hold up. There are five key leadership elements at the core of the Heart-Centered Leadership model:

1. **Trust** is being able to believe in the honesty and reliability of someone. This is built through acting consistently, following

through on commitments, and demonstrating integrity; it enables people to feel safe to do their best work.

2. **Genuineness** in a person is defined as being exactly what you appear to be. Being true to yourself and leading with sincerity builds deeper connections and ultimately stronger teams.

3. **Respect** is shown by valuing each team member's contributions, ideas, and individuality. Authentically listening, appreciating diverse perspectives, and treating others with dignity creates empowered and inclusive workplaces.

4. **Transparency** is demonstrated by sharing thoughts and opinions honestly and respectfully, building credibility and creating the conditions for honest dialogue. Transparency ensures that people have all the information they need to be successful.

5. **Vulnerability** is defined as being exposed to the possibility of being hurt or attacked. Leaders who embody this by admitting their mistakes and acknowledge they don't have all the answers create a space for collaboration and problem-solving.

This model isn't simply about leadership strategies; it's a way of being. It rejects rigid, outdated methods in favor of a people-first philosophy. It shifts from authority to service, from control to support. It's empowering. As you think about what you have read in this chapter so far, ask yourself:

- How do I currently show support to my team?
- Am I honestly serving those I lead, or am I seeking to be served?

So why do I consider myself to be a heart-centered leader? It starts with self-awareness.

I grew up in a challenging family environment, navigated male-dominated workplaces, and faced more than my fair share of toxic leadership and workplace bullying. Through all of it, I learned to reflect on how my actions impacted others as I saw how other people's actions impacted me. More importantly, I learned that compassion—both for myself and others—is nonnegotiable in leadership and life. I also embrace vulnerability, which isn't always easy.

> **Definition: Toxic leadership** is a pattern of behavior that harms employees and the organization.

I don't pretend to have all the answers. I'm not perfect, and I don't need to be. Many of us feel the need to be perfect, but it is impossible to achieve. What I am is open to learning, adapting, and growing.

I remember one particular moment when my team gave me honest feedback about my communication style during a fast-paced project. At first, it stung. I paused. Instead of getting defensive, I listened, reflected, and adjusted. Almost immediately, I saw a shift in team morale and collaboration. That experience reinforced something I already knew: leaders have a responsibility to set expectations, but they have a greater responsibility to model them. It was a reminder that leadership isn't about me. It's about the people I serve and support.

The Core Five

Before we dive into the five core elements, I want to pause and highlight a common thread: communication. You can't build trust without honest conversations. You can't show respect without really listening. You can't be genuine, transparent, or vulnerable without intentionality in how you show up. Communication is the thread that holds the leadership elements together. It's how we connect and bring heart-centered leadership to life. Now, let's look a little deeper at the five key elements that intertwine to form the heart of heart-centered leadership.

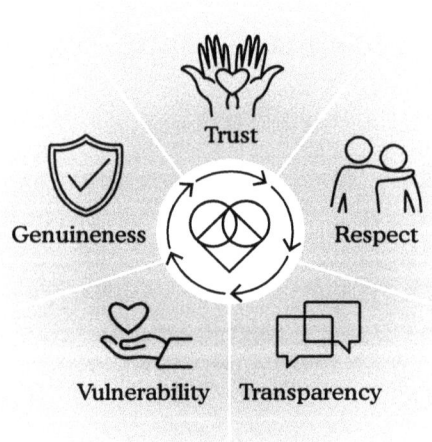

Figure 6: The Core Five

THE BLUEPRINT FOR JANE'S APPROACH TO LEADERSHIP

Trust—The Foundation of Everything

If there's one thing you absolutely can't lead without, it's trust. It's the foundation of every great team, every strong relationship, and every thriving workplace. Without it, everything crumbles. Heart-centered leaders don't demand trust—they earn it by being open and honest and by treating people with genuine respect. They don't lead from ego or fear. Instead, they create spaces where people feel safe to be themselves, experiment, and grow.

Trust isn't automatic with everyone, rather it's built through consistent actions, and as a leader you need to set the tone with how you listen, how you communicate, how consistently you show up for your people. If you're closed off, unavailable, or playing power games, don't expect your team to trust you. However, if you're present, transparent, and reliable, trust will follow.

Trust in leadership is also about trusting your team: showing them you have faith in their work and integrity and that you believe they will act with good intentions. Trusting them doesn't mean giving blind approval—they'll still need coaching and accountability—but it does mean assuming positive intent first.

A perfect example? I hold my one-on-one meetings with my team members from a place of service, always asking, "What can I do to help you keep being successful?" One of my former managers, on the other hand, led from a place of fear, using one-on-ones to criticize, control, and undermine. Trust simply couldn't exist in that environment. Patrick Lencioni, in his work on leadership and teams, says it best: "Trust is about having confidence in your team members' intentions—knowing that you don't need to protect yourself from them."

That's what real trust looks like. When you lead with genuineness and vulnerability, you create an environment where trust grows naturally and from there, everything else becomes possible.

Genuineness—You Can't Fake Leadership

If trust is the foundation, then genuineness is the glue that holds everything together. People can spot a fake leader a mile away. They might not always be able to explain why something feels off, but they feel it and know when you're not being real with them. Genuineness isn't about being perfect; it's about being real. People instinctively know when a leader shows up authentically or when they're putting on a mask. I once had a boss who said, "I don't know how to describe authenticity, but I know when I'm not getting it." He was right—you can't fake being genuine. No amount of leadership jargon or motivational posters can make up for a leader who isn't real. Genuineness means

- owning your mistakes, even when it's uncomfortable
- saying what you mean and meaning what you say
- treating people with honesty and respect, especially when the conversations are tough

One of the hardest but most valuable lessons I learned about genuineness came when I made a bad hire. The person made a great first impression, said all the right things, and on paper, seemed like a perfect fit. Over time, I began hearing rumors about his poor behavior and lack of results. I wanted to believe it would work out. I kept giving him chances, but in the end, it wasn't working; the truth became unavoidable. At that point, I had a choice. I could cover it up, pretend everything was fine, and quietly move on, or I could own the mistake. I chose to own it. I brought my team together, admitted my mistake, and gave them a once-off opportunity to be brutally honest. By doing that, I didn't lose credibility, I gained it. My team saw that I am what I am, and I am willing to own my decisions, learn from them, and create a culture of being genuine. It took courage.

Instead of replacing the vacant position, we worked together to redistribute the responsibilities across the team; it made us stronger as a team.

Being genuine isn't about always having the right answers. Instead, it's creating a culture where honesty, learning, and real conversations are the norm rather than the exception.

Respect—The Power of Making People Feel Seen

You can't talk about trust and genuineness without talking about respect. Respect is more than politeness and surface-level manners, it's fairly recognizing the value that every person brings to the table. Respect shows up in the big things and the small things.

It's how you listen.

It's how you acknowledge *effort*, not *outcomes*.

It's how you create space for different voices, even when they're quieter or different from your own.

I learned this lesson early in my leadership journey when I worked with an incredibly talented but introverted team member. He had brilliant ideas, but he rarely spoke up. It would have been easy to overlook him, to let the louder voices dominate. Instead, I made a conscious effort to create space for him to contribute. I checked in with him one-on-one. I directly encouraged him to share his ideas in meetings, and I made sure he knew that his contributions were wanted and valued.

The result was that his confidence skyrocketed. He became one of our most valuable voices, and his contributions ended up reshaping a major element of the project. That experience reinforced something huge for me: when leaders show respect, people step up, take pride in their work and are more engaged. They trust the process, and they trust themselves. In an environment of psychological safety, when people feel respected, they feel safe. They're likely to share ideas, speak up when something isn't working, and experiment without fear of judgment. You don't have to agree with every idea to respect the person sharing it. You show respect by genuinely listening, considering their perspective, and responding thoughtfully.

In one of my past roles, where I led an important project, I made it a priority to respect all contributors by acknowledging every voice in the brainstorming sessions, including (especially) junior employees. One idea that came from a junior staff member who was hesitant to even speak ended up streamlining one of our biggest processes and saving us significant time and resources. That win wouldn't have happened if I hadn't created a respectful, open environment.

Respect breathes life into innovation, growth, and belonging.

Without it, people shrink.

With it, people rise.

Transparency—Say What You Mean, Mean What You Say

If trust is the foundation, and genuineness and respect are building blocks, then transparency is the open window that lets everyone see clearly what's really going on.

Transparency is one of the quickest ways to build, or destroy, trust. When leaders are transparent, they create a sense of stability and fairness, even when the news isn't good. When they hide information, sugarcoat the truth, or manipulate facts, they breed suspicion and disengagement. Transparency is about sharing information and setting clear expectations, owning up to challenges, and creating open dialogue about

▸ where things are going well and where they aren't

- what the vision is and what the roadblocks might be
- what you expect and what people can count on from you

One of the worst leadership experiences I had was with a boss who preached trust but kept everything in silos. In our one-on-ones, she would gossip about other executives. It didn't take much imagination to realize she was probably talking about me in the same way. That behavior completely destroyed trust, ultimately poisoning the whole culture.

On the flip side, I've been lucky enough to work with a leader who modeled real transparency. He didn't pretend everything was perfect, didn't hoard information to protect power, and he shared his challenges openly to invite genuine input. We didn't always agree, but because there was openness and trust, we could have hard conversations without fear.

Transparency and communication are inseparable; it's how you set expectations, how you navigate conflict, and how you invite ownership and engagement. A culture of transparency starts at the top. If you want your people to be open with you, start by being open with them. Say what you mean. Mean what you say. Don't be afraid to tell the whole story—even when it's messy. People don't need perfect leaders; they need honest ones.

Vulnerability—The Courage to Be Real

Of all the elements of heart-centered leadership, vulnerability is commonly the one that makes people the most uncomfortable and fearful. There's still a popular opinion that vulnerability makes leaders weak. That if you admit you don't have all the answers, you'll lose authority.

The truth is exactly the opposite: vulnerability strengthens leadership. Being vulnerable as a leader means honesty about what you don't know. It means owning mistakes without defensiveness, asking for help when you need it, and listening without pretending to have it figured out.

I'll be honest, this was one of the hardest lessons for me. Early in my career, especially as a female in a male-dominated environment, I was under enormous constant pressure to prove myself. I thought that uncertainty would be seen as a lack of capability, and if I let my guard down even for a moment, I would lose credibility.

What I eventually learned, through many uncomfortable moments, was that the best leaders aren't the ones who pretended to have all the answers. They're the ones who create space for collaboration, creativity, and shared problem-solving, learning right alongside their teams.

Vulnerability definitely doesn't mean oversharing every personal detail or becoming emotionally raw in every meeting. It means showing up as human. It means saying things like:

- "I don't have all the answers yet, but I trust we can figure this out together."
- "I made a mistake, and here's what I'm doing to make it right."
- "I'm feeling challenged by this change too. Let's talk about how we can navigate it."

When leaders show vulnerability, it gives everyone permission to be genuine. It builds psychological safety, strengthens connection, and deepens trust faster than any leadership workshop or motivational speech ever could. It can be uncomfortable, because it takes real courage to lead without the armor. Those leaders who find that courage are the ones people will follow. Because they want to.

A Tale of Two CEOs

As I reflected on my experiences with two of my previous CEOs, I started to unpack why one of them successfully built the key elements of heart-centered leadership (CEO-A), while the other completely failed (CEO-B). At first glance, they both held the same title in similar-sized organizations, but the way they led, the way they communicated, and the impact they had on their teams were worlds apart.

Let's break it down.

CEO-A did something simple yet powerful—he shared the *what* and the *why* behind his decisions. Was communication always perfect? No, but ambiguity was rare. There was no need to second-guess hidden agendas because there weren't any. His transparency made me feel valued, included, and trusted. It encouraged partnership, not simple compliance, and I sincerely believe that working together strengthened the organization.

There was accountability. The buck always stopped with CEO-A. He didn't pass blame. He didn't throw his team under the bus when things went wrong. If something wasn't working, he'd have a direct, constructive conversation with me—but it never seemed like an attack or a blame game. That set the tone for the rest of us. Because he took ownership for the outcomes of the work we were doing, I felt safe to admit when I got something wrong, ask for clarity when I needed it, and—most importantly—lead my own team without fear of failure. That's what happens in a culture of trust.

Contrast that with CEO-B, who had a very different approach. He was highly directive, but somehow, when things went south, it was never his fault. He found someone else to blame. Even when he was the one making the calls, he made sure there was a scapegoat lined up. He led through control, not collaboration, which meant he didn't build real buy-in or trust. His refusal to take ownership created an environment where mistakes weren't learning opportunities—they were landmines.

That brings me to the biggest difference: the listening gap. If I had to pick one thing that truly separated these two leaders, it would be *their willingness to listen.*

CEO-A actually listened. He took the time to hear my concerns, my team's feedback, and the ideas we brought to the table. Even if he didn't always agree, we knew we were heard and respected. That mattered. It made us feel like our input was valued and we were part of something bigger. CEO-B? He *pretended* to listen. He would invite input, nod along, act like he was considering different viewpoints, and then dismiss everything and do it his way. Every. Single. Time. You know what happens when leaders do this repeatedly? People stop engaging, and culture dies.

It didn't take long for my fellow executives to figure out that giving input was a waste of time. Instead, we all defaulted to the path of least resistance—asking CEO-B what he wanted and then simply agreeing. It wasn't collaboration. It wasn't innovation. It was to avoid being a target. Let's be honest—there was nothing genuine about it.

I share this comparison because it highlights the fundamental difference between people who lead from the heart and fear-based, directive leadership.

- **Genuine leaders build strong foundations.** They prioritize trust, respect, and transparency, which leads to engaged teams, productive dynamics, and long-term success.

- **Fear-based leaders undermine their teams.** They dismiss input, evade responsibility, and create an environment of uncertainty, which ultimately weakens morale, trust, and effectiveness.

The lesson? People don't follow a job title. They follow leaders they trust, respect, and believe in. What kind of leader are you going to choose to be?

At the end of the day, trust, genuineness, respect, transparency, and vulnerability aren't merely words—they're daily actions. You can't fake this stuff. You either live it, or you don't. If you're leading with ego, fear, or control, people will feel it. So, ask yourself:

- Am I leading in a way that builds trust?
- Am I showing up as my genuine self?
- Do my people feel respected and valued?
- Am I being transparent, even when it's uncomfortable?
- Am I willing to be vulnerable and admit when I don't have all the answers?

That's what real leadership looks like. It's a choice we get to make—every single day.

> **Statistics:** According to FlairHR, 50% of CEOs struggle with developing the next generation of leaders, and only 12% of companies have confidence in their bench strength. Just 46% of leaders trust their direct manager completely, and even fewer, less than one in three, trust senior leaders in their organization.

What Happens When Leaders Lead with Heart

One of the most important outcomes of leading from the heart is that it creates emotionally engaged employees—people who aren't only showing up to do their jobs but who actually care about the work they do. When people feel connected—not only to their work, but to their leaders—they don't do the minimum. They give more. They take ownership. They go above and beyond—not because they're forced to, but because they genuinely want to.

I've seen this play out time and time again. When leaders focus solely on results without considering the people driving those results, engagement plummets and people start doing the least possible. Today's most successful leaders know they have a dual responsibility:

- deliver results

- lead a motivated, connected, and inspired workforce

This isn't optional anymore. It's a necessity. Employees today want more than a paycheck: they want purpose, they want to feel valued. They want to work for leaders who see them as people, not workers. This is where heart-centered leadership shines, at its core—it's about *empowerment*.

Empowerment isn't about giving people tasks and stepping back. It's about giving them the tools, autonomy, and confidence to excel, trusting them to take ownership of their work and supporting them so they know they're never alone. True empowerment is about creating an environment where people feel safe to take initiative, experiment, and be confident in their abilities. I've seen firsthand how transformative this can be.

One of my most rewarding moments as a leader came when I assigned an important initiative to a team member. She was tasked with leading change, and while excited, she was also hesitant and worried she wouldn't meet expectations. I assured her I wasn't expecting perfection. I was expecting her to try, learn, and grow. I did what I believe every leader should do—I gave her guidance, resources, and support, but I also stepped back and trusted her to lead. Not only did she meet my expectations, she exceeded them.

She introduced fresh ideas that became standard practice for future initiatives. That experience was a turning point for her confidence, and for me, it was an effective reminder of what happens when you correctly empower people. Let's address what empowerment isn't—because it's usually misunderstood.

I've seen far too many leaders think empowerment means delegation only. It doesn't and when it is done poorly, it can actually do more harm than good. Here are three common mistakes I've seen:

- **Lack of Clarity.** If people aren't clear on expectations, they feel lost and uncertain
- **Uneven Distribution of Responsibility.** Handing off tasks to unprepared team members sets them up for failure
- **Over-Empowerment.** Giving people full autonomy without support leads to chaos and confusion

I've learned that empowerment isn't about stepping away—it's about stepping aside and allowing team members to step up. It's about creating an environment where autonomy and guidance coexist—where people have the freedom to take initiative, but also know they aren't alone. That's something command-and-control leaders completely miss.

If empowerment is so compelling, why don't more leaders embrace it? Because true empowerment requires leaders to let go of control. For some, that's uncomfortable and terrifying. Many leaders are taught that control equals effectiveness. They think that if they're not overseeing every detail, things will fall apart. That if they are not involved in every decision they won't be seen as a strong leader, and if they don't micromanage everything, things will not go the way they want them to. I know this mindset all too well.

Growing up in a household ruled by control, I learned early what it was like to be disempowered. My independence was stifled, my opinions were questioned, and my confidence was constantly undermined. Approval always felt conditional, and love felt like something I had to earn by meeting expectations I had no say in. That experience shaped me in ways I didn't even realize at first. Instead of repeating that pattern, I made a conscious decision that I would lead differently. I would create an environment where people were safe to think for themselves, experiment, and grow without fear of punishment. My resolve strengthened as I moved into leadership roles, where I saw shocking similarities between toxic family dynamics and toxic workplaces. Command-and-control leaders had the same traits as my dad. They silenced autonomy. They suppressed independent thinking. They made leadership about their own authority rather than the success of their teams. I knew that if I wanted to create real change, I had to reject the control model and embrace trust, vulnerability, and respect. But even as I worked hard to lead this way, I found myself disempowered.

In one of my leadership roles, I built a high-performing team. I empowered them, supported them, and created a culture of trust and accountability. By contrast, I wasn't getting the same treatment from above. Instead of support, I got micromanagement and exclusion. Instead of being trusted as a leader, I found myself dictated to by my boss and certain executives that were befriended by the boss. Sycophants eager to please and make their lives easier, creating a culture of inequity and favoritism. This toxic environment extended beyond favoritism; it was political maneuvring. I saw key information withheld, not to protect the company, but to control people. The worst moment was when I was barred from doing a job I was highly qualified for, simply because the CEO wanted to bring in a friend—at an unreasonably high salary—claiming the role required "specialist knowledge." This was disempowerment at its peak.

It was a reminder that no matter how much you try to build empowerment within your own team, if the leadership above you doesn't embrace it, it will always be an uphill battle. Empowerment isn't simply a feel-good concept or a trendy word, it's a deliberate leadership choice that results from acting with trust, respect, genuineness, transparency and vulnerability. At the end of the day, empowerment is about one simple message:

THE BLUEPRINT FOR JANE'S APPROACH TO LEADERSHIP

"I believe in you."

When people feel that belief, it has a massive ripple effect. They rise. They lead. They succeed.

So does your organization.

> "Leading with integrity and empathy requires vision and a connection to your deepest self."
>
> —Karla McLaren, emotions and empathy expert

Figure 6: My first day of high school

> "The role you play as a leader is helping people experience relatedness at work: caring about and feeling cared about, feeling connected without ulterior motives, and contributing to something greater than oneself."
>
> —Susan Fowler, founder and CEO of Mojo Moments

THE BLUEPRINT FOR JANE'S APPROACH TO LEADERSHIP

Lavinia's Story: A Journey on her Own Terms

Lavinia is a consultant, a business owner, and an immigrant. Her journey has been shaped by experiences of displacement, self-discovery, and an unyielding commitment to designing a life on her own terms.

Born to American parents, Lavinia emigrated to New Zealand at twelve, an experience that made her acutely aware of what it felt like to be different. Childhood was isolating, but it also sparked a deep introspection that shaped her future. "I was not going to settle in any way," she says. "I've designed a life on my own terms." She followed her heart wherever it led—working in media across the US and Europe, traveling extensively, and immersing herself in her passions: writing, reading, and publishing. Above all, she loved people—their stories, their experiences, their struggles. "Interviewing people and hearing their stories remains one of my greatest joys," she shares. Combining these passions, she built a business that gives her fulfillment every day.

Returning to New Zealand after years abroad, Lavinia was driven by a desire to make a difference. She found a role at a nonprofit, interviewing vulnerable families living in poverty, documenting their stories to pitch to the media and raise awareness. She threw herself into the work, staying late, learning everything she could, and making a real impact. Her efforts resulted in significant media coverage for the charity, amplifying the voices of those in need. Feeling inspired, Lavinia took on a side project in her own time—something that aligned with the charity's mission but was entirely self-driven. "I didn't tell anyone," she recalls. "I worked on it during my evenings and weekends, and when it was ready, I approached the second in charge, the Chief Operating Officer (COO), for support."

The COO was enthusiastic, agreeing to help implement the project while respecting Lavinia's intellectual property. However, before anything could be formalized, the COO left the organization, leaving Lavinia at the mercy of a very different kind of leader.

Facing Narcissistic Leadership

The CEO at the time, she now realizes, was a textbook narcissist: full of self-importance and lacking any form of empathy. Back then, she didn't have the language to describe his behavior, but she knew something was wrong. When she approached him about the project and the verbal agreement she had made, he literally laughed in her face.

"I had made a mistake—I launched the project before getting a signed written agreement," she reflects. "The organization received a great deal of publicity; we were on TVNZ, and in major newspapers—it was one of the happiest times of my life." The CEO did not share in the celebration. When she excitedly showed him what the organization had achieved and asked if he was proud of it, his response was a chilling "No." Looking back, she sees it for what it was—intense jealousy. The success wasn't about him; it was about the organization, and worse, about her. That wasn't acceptable.

She asked him again to sign the agreement, and his response was absolute: "We own the intellectual property. It belongs to the organization."

Lavinia pushed back. "Absolutely not. I did this 100 percent in my own time." That was the moment everything changed. For the next six months, she became the target of a relentless campaign. He set her up to fail, assigning her tasks she was unqualified for, such as legal work and complex accounting. When she sought help from HR, they quietly told her, "You do realize you're being set up to fail?"

The emotional toll was immense. She became depressed, exhausted by his relentless tactics of undermining her and keeping her off balance. One moment, he would throw uninvited compliments her way: "Sorry, I got distracted, you're so beautiful." The next, he would launch targeted attacks: "You know you're a Lone Ranger here, don't you? You work in isolation." It wasn't until friends pointed it out that she fully grasped what was happening. "You can see that this is bullying and sexual harassment, right?" they asked. How right they were.

One day she noticed that the CEO was holed up in his office with lawyers, facing bullying and harassment complaints from other employees. As much as Lavinia wanted to share her own experience, she remained silent. "I was too scared to share what was happening to me in case it affected my future," she admits. Through it all, she refused to back down. "It was the only source of power and control I had left," she says. The CEO needed her work, and she leveraged that. Every time he asked for urgent reports he required, she responded, "I'll give them to you when you sign the agreement." When he had another manager check in on what work she had done, she replied, "Oh, that's easy—nothing."

She made waves. Eventually, the pressure worked. One Friday, after a boozy lunch, the CEO called her up. "If you come to my office now, I'll sign your agreement." She didn't hesitate. She walked into his office, grabbed the signed document, and left without another word. "Finally," she thought, but the moment of victory was overshadowed by exhaustion and anger. Shortly after that, she left the job, shattered but free.

The experience broke her. It took months to recover from the damage inflicted by that commanding leadership model. She never looked back, and she never worked in that corporate model again. After leaving, Lavinia became a consultant. "After that experience, it was all on my terms," she says. "No one will ever do that to me again."

Her first consulting role was with a female director—an experience that opened her eyes to a different kind of leadership. "It was the opposite of what I had endured," she explains. "It was collaborative, not top-down. It was about genuine connection, authenticity, and emotional intelligence."

She soaked up everything she could. Now, as a business owner, she leads with those same principles. "Everything I do for my clients and team members is heart centered. It's not about control; it's about trust and empowerment."

The Future of Leadership

Lavinia believes that the corporate model, as it exists today, is unsustainable. "Women have woken up," she says. "We recognize what constitutes abuse, and we no longer tolerate it." Looking back, she and her colleagues didn't have the language to describe what they experienced under that toxic CEO. "We knew we felt uncomfortable, but we didn't know why. Now we do."

The shift is happening. Leadership is evolving. Lavinia stands firm in her belief that the future belongs to those who lead with integrity, emotional awareness, and genuine care for others.

3

The Hidden Ingredients of Great Leadership

Psychological Safety: The Secret Sauce

Psychological safety is the foundation of a thriving workplace. It's what allows people to experiment, voice their ideas, and test their potential—all without fear of judgment or reprisal. It's what enables teams to innovate, collaborate, and grow rather than shutting down in fear or uncertainty.

Psychological safety is cyclic in nature: it isn't simply a byproduct of great leadership—it's also what makes great leadership possible. The five key elements of my heart-centered leadership model—trust, genuineness, respect, transparency, and vulnerability—intertwine, as do the two environmental factors that hold everything together: psychological safety and emotional intelligence.

When leaders prioritize psychological safety, they create the conditions for the key elements to flourish. And when they lead with the key elements, they create psychological safety. It's a feedback loop—one that, when done right, transforms workplaces from toxic and fear-driven into collaborative, innovative, and engaged environments.

Psychological safety has become a bit of a buzzword lately, but it's so much more than a trendy leadership concept. It's the difference between a high-performing team and a dysfunctional one. When it is absent, a toxic culture is created—one where fear takes over, voices go silent, and trust crumbles. People prioritize protecting themselves over contributing to meaningful work. Psychological safety is about creating an environment where people feel secure enough to be themselves and experiment with new concepts.

While leaders play a crucial role, psychological safety shouldn't depend solely on one person. The real power lies in embedding it into the culture, making it sustainable and self-reinforcing. It should be built into the fabric of the organization so it persists beyond any one leader's presence. When this is achieved, organizations have a massive advantage. They

- **reframe mistakes as learning opportunities**, encouraging innovation with a proactive approach to problem-solving and continuous improvement
- **promote collaboration**, enhancing problem-solving and decision-making through diverse perspectives and teamwork
- **boost engagement**, valuing, including, and connecting people, which increases productivity and retention and enhances overall business performance

For me, it's deeply personal and hits incredibly close to home.

I never experienced it as a child. Growing up in an environment where I never felt safe, where I constantly walked on eggshells, shaped my understanding of how essential emotional safety is. In my childhood, fear dictated behavior. Having a narcissistic parent meant that mistakes weren't merely discouraged—they were met with anger, judgment, and ridicule. There was no space to ask questions, no room to challenge authority, and no possibility of being vulnerable.

So I adapted. I learned to hide my vulnerabilities, to make myself invisible and to suppress my voice—because speaking up time and again made matters worse. The result? A paralyzing sense of insecurity that followed me into adulthood, making me deeply aware of how a lack of psychological safety erodes confidence, stifles creativity, and crushes self-worth.

When I entered the workforce, I saw the same dynamics play out in command-and-control leadership environments. Teams held back, fearful of how their ideas would be received. People didn't challenge the status quo, even when they knew something wasn't working. Leaders ruled with intimidation rather than inclusion, and as a result, innovation suffered, collaboration was minimal, and trust was nonexistent.

I also saw something else. I saw what happened when leaders build cultures of safety. I saw teams succeed, ideas flourish, and people bring their full selves to work. I saw the power of workplaces that encouraged open dialogue, embraced mistakes as learning moments, and prioritized respect over control. This reinforced my core belief that psychological safety isn't optional—it's essential. It's arguably, the single most influential factor that determines whether teams reach their full potential or crumble under pressure. When people perform rather than crumble, they handle the unexpected and the ambiguity of change; they are able to see the bigger picture.

One moment that stands out for me happened when I was leading a major organizational change in a government department. The change impacted multiple teams, requiring extensive consultation across different levels—from frontline administrators to senior executives and external stakeholders. It was a system change project that required full buy-in and collaboration, but there was a roadblock. One of the key stakeholders, someone whose input was critical to the success of the project, was incredibly resistant to the change. Her fear and frustration started spreading to the rest of the team, creating unnecessary tension, which was threatening to delay the project.

At first, I approached the situation logically. I had multiple conversations with her and her manager, hoping to help her understand the long-term benefits of the new system. No matter how rational my arguments were, her resistance only deepened. Then, I stepped back, asked myself what was really going on, and had an *aha!* moment. I was focusing on the process, not the person. After another honest conversation, I learned that her resistance had nothing to do with the system itself. Her homelife was unstable and abusive, and work had become her safe space. The idea of major changes at work was triggering increasing instability in an already fragile situation. So, instead of pushing her to get on board, I asked a different question:

"What would make you feel safe throughout this process?"

By shifting the conversation from compliance to care, everything changed. Together, we worked out a solution that allowed her to temporarily transfer to another department where she could maintain stability while the transition happened. Once the change was fully implemented, she returned on her own terms, without the added stress of feeling like she had no control over the situation. The roadblock disappeared; the project was back on track. The team moved forward. She felt safe.

This example demonstrates that psychological safety isn't about coddling people or avoiding challenges. It's about understanding what people need to feel secure enough to show up fully, engage openly, and perform at their best. It's about creating environments where people don't have to hold their breath, walk on eggshells, or protect themselves from leadership. That's the power of leading from a place of trust, respect, transparency, vulnerability, and genuine care.

Some of the Research Out There

Before we look at practical ways of creating psychological safety, let's look at what the experts say.

The concept of psychological safety isn't new. It was initially the brainchild of Harvard's Amy Edmondson, who has spent decades researching what makes teams measurably effective. Edmondson's research, along with a Google study known as Project Aristotle, show that psychological safety is the number one factor in high-performing teams. When people feel psychologically safe, they're inclined to innovate, collaborate, learn from each other, and own up to mistakes before they become costly. It's the difference between a team that plays not to lose, and one that plays to win.

Recent studies back this up. A 2023 article in *The Open Psychology Journal* found that psychological safety has a significant influence on team dynamics, which in turn affects team learning, efficiency, and productivity. The study concluded that promoting psychological safety is essential for team success and serves as a foundation for modern organizations. Another study published in *Frontiers in Psychology* explored how psychological safety influences team efficacy; it showed enhanced learning behavior and overall team effectiveness, especially when combined with strong leadership and clear communication.

Psychological safety has been linked to increased innovation within teams. According to a study highlighted in the *Journal of Organizational Behavior,* psychological safety serves as an effective moderator between process innovation and performance. The cooperative environment fostered by psychological safety encourages the sharing of ideas, which is crucial for successful innovation. Similarly, research in the *Creativity Research Journal* indicates that inclusive leadership enhances employee involvement in creative tasks. When leaders are open and available to listen, employees feel safe to share new ideas, thereby increasing creativity within the team.

Speaking of leadership—this is where the rubber really hits the road. Leaders either make or break a psychologically safe culture. Research published by the Harvard Business School outlines four steps that leaders can take to cultivate a culture of safety; in the next section we will explore Timothy R. Clark's four-stage framework and my reflections from my experience.

Firstly, a caution: research from the Wharton School reminds us that too much psychological safety, without clear expectations or accountability, can lead to complacency. So, like anything, balance is key. The best leaders create environments where people feel safe and are held to a high standard.

How to Build a Fear-Free Workplace: The Four Stages

Timothy R. Clark's four sequential stages of psychological safety provide an effective framework for embedding this essential cultural element into the workplace. These stages resonate with me, as they represent the exact opposite of what I experienced growing up, what I endured in controlling workplace environments, and what I witnessed from bullying leaders who stifled growth.

For me, it is very personal. It's about breaking cycles of fear and control and replacing them with conditions that result in empowerment, innovation, and resilience. It's also the critical link between my heart-centered leadership model and the environment that sustains it. Let's break down Timothy R. Clark's four stages of psychological safety and explore how it plays out in the real world.

> **Definition: Resilience** is successfully adapting to difficult or challenging life experiences.

Stage 1: Inclusion Safety

This first stage ensures that everyone feels a sense of belonging, regardless of background, identity, or experience. It's about creating an inclusive environment where diversity is not only acknowledged but valued and celebrated.

My Reflection: Growing up, I rarely felt like I belonged. I think many children experience moments of feeling invisible, but in my case, with a narcissistic dad, I generally felt like a burden rather than a valued part of the family. I learned to stay small, to be invisible, and to avoid drawing attention that might invite criticism. Later, when I stepped into male-dominated workplaces, I experienced a different kind of exclusion. I was frequently left out of key conversations and treated as the token female in leadership discussions. When I was included, it seemed performative rather than genuine.

These experiences shaped me into a person who is deliberate about inclusion and acts with genuine care about people. I never want anyone on my team to feel invisible or that they don't matter. I've learned that recognizing and celebrating each person's uniqueness results in strengthened teams. When people feel fairly seen and valued, they contribute more, collaborate better, and feel a stronger connection to their work and their teams.

Stage 2: Learner Safety

Learner safety means creating an environment where people feel safe to ask questions, make mistakes, and seek feedback without fear of embarrassment or punishment. It's about reframing failure—not as something to be avoided, but as an essential step in learning and growth.

My Reflection: I've seen firsthand what happens when teams feel safe to learn. One particular project stands out. My team was struggling to stay on time to deliver a complex project that hit multiple roadblocks. Instead of hiding mistakes or staying silent, people were comfortable speaking up, sharing concerns, and brainstorming solutions together to get us back on track.

On the flip side, I've also witnessed the devastating effects of a fear-based culture. I once worked in an organization where a junior marketing professional made an error that had organization-wide implications. Instead of owning up to it immediately, she tried to cover it up. Why? Because she knew that admitting a mistake would lead to public humiliation rather than constructive feedback. When the truth finally surfaced, her manager vilified her for the initial mistake, rather than asking the real question: *Why did she feel so unsafe that she had to hide it in the first place?* By failing to reflect and instead reinforcing a culture of blame, that manager ensured that others in the team would continue to operate in fear. Organizations that honestly embrace learner safety don't punish mistakes—they analyze them, learn from them, and grow because of them.

Stage 3: Contributor Safety

This stage builds on learner safety, allowing individuals to apply their skills, take initiative, and actively participate without fear of getting it "wrong." It's about trusting people to do their jobs—and empowering them to step into their strengths.

My Reflection: I've worked with many brilliant but hesitant individuals—people who had all the skills and knowledge but lacked the confidence or opportunity to contribute. One of the most impactful transformations I've witnessed involved a highly skilled, introverted team member. She had been consistently overlooked and even dismissed because her work told the real story—not the story leadership wanted to hear. She had learned to stay quiet rather than challenge the narrative. When I took over the team, I saw her potential immediately. I gave her ownership of reporting within an agreed framework, then supported her as she presented her findings in meetings. At first, I attended with her, offering reinforcement, but over time, as her confidence grew, I gradually stepped back. The change was remarkable. Once hesitant and overlooked, she became a respected authority in her field. Contributor safety gave her the freedom to stand in her expertise without fear. That's the real power of the contributor safety stage: when people feel respected and trusted, they step up in incredible ways.

Stage 4: Challenger Safety

The final stage of psychological safety is challenger safety—where individuals feel secure enough to question ideas, challenge the status quo, and offer constructive criticism without fear of retaliation. This is the stage that enables true innovation, meaningful progress, and transformational change.

My Reflection: Growing up, challenging authority was discouraged, and it was dangerous behavior. The consequences of speaking up in my childhood were unpredictable, leading to hesitation, self-doubt, and silence. It took years for me to unlearn that fear and develop the confidence to challenge the status quo. As a leader, I prioritize creating spaces where my teams feel safe to challenge ideas—including my own. Some of the most game-changing transformations I've witnessed have come from team members who felt empowered to question outdated processes, propose alternatives, and push for better solutions. Not all leaders welcome this kind of thinking; some view questions as threats. They mistake constructive conversations for insubordination. They see alternative viewpoints as personal attacks. Over time, this creates a stagnant culture—one where employees stop thinking critically, stop contributing, and ultimately disengage.

In contrast, leaders who embrace challenger safety actively invite diverse perspectives, listen without defensiveness, and reward critical thinking. They understand that strong teams agree, but they also challenge each other in ways that makes everyone better.

A Cautionary Tale: CEO-A versus CEO-B

This is where my experience with CEO-A and CEO-B becomes increasingly relevant. CEO-A actively developed challenger safety. He encouraged open discussions, welcomed different perspectives, and valued honest dialogue. His leadership created a culture of psychological safety where questioning led to progress, not punishment. CEO-B, on the other hand, went through the motions of listening, but not from a place of genuineness. Instead, he used team discussions as intelligence-gathering exercises—later weaponizing the information against employees. Rather than strengthening trust, his actions eroded it completely. That is the danger of false psychological safety—when leaders pretend to welcome input but ultimately use it to maintain control.

Leaders who authentically embrace building a culture of psychological safety don't simply lead. They elevate.

Practical Ways to Make Your Team Feel Safe, Valued, and Heard

Let's be really honest with ourselves: psychological safety doesn't organically happen. It's not a policy, a one-time initiative, or a workplace trend. It's a commitment, a daily practice, that must be actively cultivated, protected, and reinforced. So how do you actually build this culture? How do you create an environment where people feel secure enough to be themselves, confident enough to contribute, and supported enough to grow?

I am not pretending to have all the answers—it's complicated—but it has to start from the top. Leadership behaviors, communication style, and decisions made or not made shape the culture.

Lead by Example: Show Up with Vulnerability

If you want your team to be open and honest, go first. Leaders who pretend to have all the answers, think they never make mistakes, and fake having everything together create a culture where people feel like they have to do the same. That's exhausting. Instead, practice genuineness. Share your failures and lessons; admit when you don't know something. Be open about challenges you've faced and share what you learned, reinforcing one of the key elements: vulnerability. This signals confidence and shows your team that perfection isn't a requirement for contribution, and that honesty is valued over appearances. With that said, vulnerability needs balance. Be mindful that sharing too much or sharing in the wrong way can undermine confidence in leadership. The goal isn't to offload personal struggles onto your team—it's to model a behavior that builds connection.

→ *What this looks like in action:* Instead of pretending you have all the answers, try saying, "I don't have the perfect solution, but let's figure it out together." That small shift changes everything.

Listen—Really Listen

Listening isn't about hearing words; it's about making people feel heard. Read that again out loud—*feel heard*. If people don't believe their input matters, they'll stop giving it. That's why active listening is one of the most robust leadership tools out there. True listening means not interrupting or dismissing ideas (even if you disagree), paying attention to what's *not* being said—body language, hesitation, tone—and asking thoughtful follow-ups, showing that you value input and that you *heard*! I've always been a huge fan of Stephen Covey's principle, "Seek first to understand, then to be understood." He talks about the five levels of listening, and let me tell you, many people never make it past the first level. I encourage you to reflect on your own listening habits. Are you clearly engaged in conversations, or are you waiting for your turn to speak? The way you listen shapes the way your team interacts with you. I have to I check myself frequently, and this makes me mindful and alert.

→ *What this looks like in action:* The next time someone brings you a concern, don't jump in with a solution. Instead, ask: "Tell me more about what's on your mind." Watch what happens. To show the person that you heard and understood, reflect back to them by paraphrasing parts of what they said.

→ *What often gets missed:* Listening alone isn't enough. To build trust, you need to act on what you've heard, whether it's a big intervention or a small acknowledgment. It might be adjusting a decision, following up, or simply letting someone know their perspective made a difference. When people feel heard, they feel valued.

Encourage Experimentation: Make Failure Safe

If people are afraid to fail, they won't innovate. Organizations that punish mistakes end up killing creativity, slowing progress, and making people hesitant to take risks. The most successful teams normalize failure as part of the learning process. I've always championed "outside-the-box" thinking in every team I've led because I've learned that innovation starts with a simple but mighty question:

"What problem are you trying to solve?"

It sounds basic, but I've seen lightbulbs go off when people finally shift from a focus on quick solutions to actually understanding the problem. I hope that I have left this legacy in every workplace. Mistakes will happen, what matters is how leaders respond. If the first reaction is criticism or blame, people will avoid experimentation. If the response is curiosity and learning, they'll feel safe enough to try again.

→ *What this looks like in action:* When something doesn't go as planned, instead of saying "Why did this fail?", try asking "What did we learn from this?" That small shift changes the conversation entirely. In fact, even when activities go as planned, it is still good practice to ask what has been learned.

Recognize Effort—Not Simply Results

Recognition is one of the simplest, yet most overlooked leadership tools. People need to know what success looks like and that their contributions matter. I'm not talking about results—I'm talking about effort, progress, and improvement. Fear-based leaders only acknowledge success. Heart-centered leaders recognize the journey, not only the outcome. However—and this is important—recognition must be genuine. People can smell fake praise a mile away. It's not about handing out compliments for the sake of it—it's about acknowledging real contributions in a respectful way.

→ *What this looks like in action:* Instead of a generic "Great job," try, "I really appreciate how you handled that tough conversation today. Your approach kept the discussion productive." Specific recognition builds confidence and reinforces positive behaviors.

Keep It Going: The Danger of Abandoning Psychological Safety

Creating psychological safety isn't about getting it right once; it's about consistency. I've seen firsthand what happens when leaders start strong but fail to follow through. At one major corporation I worked in, a forward-thinking executive launched a well-being program consisting of meditation sessions, early-finish Fridays and team-building activities. The shift in culture was tangible, morale improved, engagement went up, and people felt valued. Unfortunately, when that executive was made redundant, the program was axed immediately. The result? Employees felt betrayed. What had once been a genuine effort to improve well-being now seemed like a short-lived corporate PR stunt. Morale didn't fall to its previous state; it plummeted below where it had started, and staff disengagement followed. This is the danger of treating psychological safety and mental well-being as a temporary initiative rather than a long-term leadership philosophy and investment in culture.

→ *What this looks like in action:* If you're going to introduce an initiative to improve culture, ask yourself: "Am I ready to commit to this for the long haul?" Because if not, the damage of starting and stopping is worse than not starting at all.

Final Thoughts: The Long-Term Impact of Psychological Safety

By maintaining momentum and committing to long-term cultural development, heart-centered leaders ensure that their efforts create lasting impact. It's about nurturing the culture continuously and consistently, even when challenges arise. This is how organizations move beyond short-term fixes and achieve sustained growth, innovation, and engagement.

When leaders commit to communicating with care, consistency, and courage, they create a culture where people feel safe to speak up and safe to stay. The wider commitment to psychological safety is an investment in the resilience of the organization, enabling strategic success, adaptability, and long-term sustainability.

Companies are facing a leadership crisis—existing leaders are frustrated and exhausted, benches are thinning out and there is a significant shortage of leaders prepared to fill key roles. In order to survive, organizations must invest in creating an environment where emerging leaders feel valued and can find purpose in their work. That means prioritizing trust, authenticity, and diversity, along with a holistic approach to career growth and development."

—Stephanie Neal, Director of DDI's Center for Analytics and Behavioral Research

Emotional Intelligence: The Nonnegotiable

In today's workplaces, Emotional Intelligence (EQ) isn't a bonus; it's an absolute necessity for a better outcome for the business. It's what separates good leaders from legitimately great ones. It allows leaders to create connection, navigate challenges, and bring out the best in their people. Coined by American psychologist Daniel Goleman, emotional intelligence is the ability to recognize, understand, and manage our own emotions while effectively responding to the emotions of others. Goleman identifies five core components of EQ:

1. **Empathy**: understanding and responding appropriately to the feelings of others
2. **Social Skills**: interacting well with other people, being able to clearly articulate thoughts while actively listening
3. **Self-Awareness**: recognizing our own emotions and their impact, recognizing the interrelatedness of how we feel and the actions we take
4. **Self-Regulation**: managing emotions in a constructive way, being flexible and managing conflict
5. **Motivation**: being internally motivated, maintaining a growth mindset and inspiring others

For heart-centered leaders, these are foundational skills. Without them, leadership becomes a transactional process rather than a transformational one. When applied to leadership, EQ is like a compass in stormy weather—helping leaders steer teams through uncertainty, conflict, and change. Leaders with high EQ create workplaces where people feel valued, heard, and safe. Their ability to manage emotions, diffuse tension, and navigate relationships allows teams to flourish. On the other hand, leaders who lack EQ create the opposite effect.

> **Definition** from *Vertical Growth* by Michael Bunting with Carl Lemieux: **Image management** refers to the time and energy we waste in organizations on blame, denial, deflection, defense, gossip, politics, saving face, masking our weaknesses, and other fear-based strategies to make ourselves feel safe or look good.

Personally, I associate a lack of EQ with bullying and narcissistic tendencies, as such individuals customarily prioritize their ego and self-image over understanding the emotions and needs of those they lead. They may appear charismatic and capable on the surface, but their lack of genuine empathy and self-awareness creates environments of fear and insecurity.

I've seen the difference firsthand. I once attended an executive meeting during a major organizational change. When the CEO walked in unannounced, the energy in the room shifted immediately. What had been a collaborative discussion suddenly turned into silent tension. People stopped sharing ideas, worried about saying the "wrong" thing in front of him. The meeting became one-sided, with the CEO dictating rather than engaging. Compare that to a different leadership team I worked with, where the senior leader's presence brought energy, warmth, and genuine curiosity. She invited open debate, asked tough questions with empathy, and genuinely listened. Instead of shutting people down, she empowered them to contribute fully.

Same type of meeting. Radically different outcomes. Both CEOs said that the conversation was in a safe space, but only one was walking the talk.

When leaders or team members lack emotional intelligence, the consequences are far-reaching.

- **Conflicts escalate**: Misunderstandings and unresolved tensions lead to mistrust, frustration, and disengagement
- **Collaboration suffers**: Instead of working together, individuals operate in silos, pushing personal agendas instead of team goals
- **Poor decision-making**: Leaders who lack self-awareness double down on failing strategies because they can't read the room or adapt, often throwing money at a problem rather than making a call
- **High turnover and lost productivity**: Emotionally draining work environments push top talent away, driving people toward organizations that prioritize empathy, trust, and purpose

Dee Harding of the Coaching Academy notes that it's no longer money or perks that drive employees; it's meaning and purpose. Leaders who prioritize EQ understand that creating a culture of mutual respect, cooperation, and trust is essential to the success of the modern workplace. Emotionally intelligent leaders understand that emotions aren't obstacles—they are actually sources of wisdom. They use this knowledge to guide decisions, inspire teams, and create a culture where people want to work. A sincerely heart-centered, emotionally intelligent leader does a few key things:

- **They create safe spaces.** They validate emotions and perspectives, ensuring people feel heard and respected.
- **They empower teams to experiment.** They encourage learning even when things don't go as planned.
- **They enhance collaboration.** Their ability to communicate effectively helps teams navigate challenges and differences with ease.
- **They remain steady in uncertainty.** Because they understand their own emotions, they don't let stress or fear dictate their leadership.

Figure 7: Mum, Christopher, and me in the concrete backyard of our terraced house in Radcliffe, England

For me, developing EQ has been a personal journey. Growing up in a household without emotional safety, I learned what happens when empathy and understanding are absent and how fear stifles confidence and self-expression. Later in my career, I witnessed workplaces that mirrored the same patterns. These experiences also shaped my commitment to leading differently, to building environments where people feel valued, understood, and supported. A heart-centered emotionally intelligent leader is transformational. They communicate with intention, guide with empathy, build trust through transparency, and create an environment where people can bring their whole selves to work.

They achieve the necessary business outcomes, but also leave a lasting, positive impact on the organization and the lives they touch.

> "Emotional Intelligence is more important than IQ in almost every role and many times more important in leadership roles"
>
> —Stephen Covey, author of *The 7 Habits of Highly Effective People*

> "The achievements of an organization are the results of the combined effort of each individual"
>
> —Vincent Lombardi, American football coach

Leading Change with Heart

If there's one thing that we can all agree on, it's that change is constant. Organizations are always evolving—whether it's a major transformation, a restructure, a shift in company culture, the adoption of new technology, or an unexpected global crisis. The technical side of change (processes, systems, structures) gets plenty of attention. What gets overlooked is the emotional side of change, and that's where the real work happens. Because change isn't only a business shift. It's a human experience. According to PROSCI's ADKAR Model, "organizational change can only happen when individuals change."

For many people, change triggers fear: fear of the unknown, fear of failure, fear of losing status or job security, fear of not being able to keep up. When fear takes hold, people do what they've been conditioned to do: they resist, they disengage, they cling to the old way of doing things, even when it no longer serves them. The difference between leaders who successfully guide teams through change and those who create chaos and disengagement comes down to the two things that we have been discussing throughout this chapter: psychological safety and emotional intelligence.

This is where heart-centered leadership becomes a game-changer. A heart-centered leader doesn't force change through control or authority. They don't pretend to have all the answers or dismiss the emotional impact of change as "part of doing business." Instead, they guide with respect and empathy. They create an environment where people feel safe enough to move forward, confident enough to question, and supported enough to navigate uncertainty. They *lead* people through it. Here's how:

Overcommunicate and Be Transparent

In times of change, you can never communicate too much. People need to know what is happening, however they really need to understand the *why*. If there's ambiguity, people fill in the gaps with assumptions and fear. Heart-centered leaders eliminate that uncertainty. They share what they know, acknowledge what they don't, and invite dialogue. Even when the full picture isn't clear, they never leave their people in the dark.

→ *What this looks like in action:* In one organization, during a major enterprise-wide restructure, I made a point of holding weekly check-ins with my team. Even when I didn't have all the answers, I was honest about what I knew and what was still unfolding. Being transparent built trust even in the middle of uncertainty.

Validate and Address Fear (Instead of Ignoring It)

Change naturally triggers fear. Leaders who ignore fear lose trust fast. Instead of minimizing concerns or brushing them aside, create space for honest conversations. Acknowledge discomfort, invite people to share what's on their minds, and respond with understanding rather than defensiveness.

→ *What this looks like in action:* In one transformation project, I had a team member who was visibly disengaged. Instead of assuming she was being difficult, I had a one-on-one conversation to understand what was holding her back. Her fear was that she wouldn't be able to keep up with the change and would be seen as obsolete. By simply listening, validating her concerns, and offering support, she reengaged with the process instead of resisting it; she saw the growth opportunity and that influenced others around her.

Reinforce Psychological Safety Through Actions (Not Just Words)

It's one thing to tell people they can be open and honest. It's another thing to prove it through leadership actions. Heart-centered leaders demonstrate psychological safety by how they respond to challenges, mistakes, and feedback. They are genuine, and they walk the talk.

→ *What this looks like in action:* I once worked on a major IT transformation project where the initial rollout experienced unexpected setbacks. The easy route would have been to blame the team and demand immediate fixes. Instead, I gathered the team and said, "OK, this didn't go as planned—what can we learn?" That shift to learning-based leadership created an environment where people felt safe to experiment, iterate, and innovate without fear of punishment. We turned that failure into one of the most successful projects I've ever led.

Celebrate Small Wins (Because Change Is a Marathon, Not a Sprint)

Change is exhausting, and if people don't see progress along the way, they lose motivation. Maintaining momentum is critical for successful change. Heart-centered leaders intentionally celebrate the small victories, the incremental steps that get the team to the big celebration at the end.

→ *What this looks like in action:* During a major organizational change, I made it a point to recognize individual and team accomplishments—no matter how small. Whether it was adapting to a new process, navigating a tough transition or having a difficult conversation, those regular moments of celebration helped sustain morale and engagement.

At the heart of each of these actions is clear, compassionate communication—because in times of change, how we speak and how we listen is as important, maybe even more, as what we do.

Your Leadership Legacy Starts Here

As we close this chapter, I want to leave you with one final thought: Impact. Leadership is about the way we make people feel, whether we inspire them to bring their full selves to work or leave them questioning their worth. Leaders are remembered for their strategies and their efficiency, but the *best leaders* are remembered for how they made people feel through moments of uncertainty, challenge, and change. In a world where change is the only constant, heart-centered leadership is an opportunity to build resilient, empowered, thriving people.

That's the kind of leadership that leaves a legacy.

Josh's Story: A Journey Through Redefining Purpose

I asked Josh for a quote to start off his story, and he said: "Do the work and let it speak for itself." As you read his journey, you'll see why this is so fitting.

Josh grew up in a small regional town where community, church, and his parents' business shaped his world. His family's farming background instilled a strong work ethic from a young age—there was always something to do. "We as kids worked, it was the natural thing to do. We learnt about business quite young," he recalls. Holidays were spent on relatives' farms, blending fun with responsibility.

His upbringing encouraged a sense of trust in people. "I never doubted people's intentions. We all helped each other," he explains. Of course, small-town politics existed, but status and influence mattered little in his world.

As he grew up, his career wasn't a structured conversation with his parents. Instead, he learned from those around him. "We didn't get pocket money—we worked for it, and we were good at it, so we kept doing it." At some point though, he realized that he was being underestimated. "I don't know what it was, but it made me determined from a relatively young age to prove people wrong."

The Reality of Working with People Who Don't Care

Fast forwarding, Josh moved to the city to attend university. "I was pretty good at most things, so I never really knew what I wanted to do." Josh's feels his biggest challenge then was finding his true passion, so instead he studied something that he knew he was good at. He approached his studies and his career with a youthful belief that anything he tried would work. Failure was never realistically considered as he set out as a freelancer. "The worst that could happen was failure, but that wasn't even in my thinking."

That mindset changed when he encountered people who took advantage of his inexperience. "A few hard lessons came from people who screwed me over under the guise of *'that's just business.'*" However, on the positive side, working for himself allowed him to choose his team, people who were skilled and committed. Eventually, as a solo operator, he hit the limits of his knowledge. "I didn't have mentors to guide me to the next stage when I needed it."

So he took a job to learn from others. That's when he faced a new challenge: working with people who simply didn't care. "Some people didn't want to be there. They'd openly resist progress and do the bare minimum." Coming from his farming roots and running his own show, where deadlines dictated everything, this was a shock. "I couldn't understand how people didn't want to do a good job."

A defining moment came when he realized that failure was

sometimes the best option. "I worked very hard to keep things alive when I should've let them die. Some people never wanted it to succeed."

Command-and-Control versus Heart-Centered Leadership

Josh experienced two types of command-and-control leadership throughout his career. One was structured yet fair, ensuring both people and outcomes were valued. The other was fear-driven, prioritizing image over impact.

"I like command-and-control leadership within the right parameters," he says. "I need to know the directive. Without it, things get messy." He thrived in environments with clear decision-making structures. "In media, you knew the chain of command. If you weren't performing, it wasn't personal; it was about the mission. No one had time to worry about who was coming at you with knives in the back; they came at you head on.

"My worst experiences were when no one could speak the truth and blind agreement was demanded, agree with the leader, or else." He saw how scapegoating thrived in toxic workplaces. "People were always looking for someone to blame. If you admitted uncertainty, they'd smell blood in the water, and they knew they could deflect the blame onto you." At times, seeking transparency made him a problem. "Asking for clarity made certain managers feel exposed. They didn't want the accountability, so they saw me as trouble."

A new hire once took his place as the office target. "For the first time, I felt safe—but also guilty because my actions contributed to that toxic culture by watching it happen." Unfortunately, she was forced out by the narcissistic manager because she refused to be broken.

Redefining Leadership

Josh aspires to be a heart-centered leader. "The leaders I admire have vision, empathy, and compassion. They're the ultimate coaches."

One manager left a lasting impression. "She supported people through their worst moments and gave them the space to succeed or fail. She had our backs." Unlike toxic workplaces where truth was dangerous, she encouraged open discussions. "We could ask her, 'We don't have control over this outcome—how should we handle it?' That wouldn't have been possible in other environments."

He sees leadership as the ultimate balancing act. "You have to deal with today's crisis while staying focused on long-term goals. The best leaders keep people anchored to a shared vision." At its core, leadership is about security. "A great leader needs to feel secure in their role to support their team. In this transactional world, that's harder than ever."

He believes leadership isn't about grand gestures but about guiding people toward a purpose. "The best leaders map out a vision, focus on the right problems, and keep people moving in the right direction." Josh's journey has made him cautious but also more strategic. He understands that not everyone works toward the same goal—but he remains hopeful. Leadership, to him, is about navigating systems, recognizing people's motivations, and staying true to the mission. Above all else, doing the work and letting it speak for itself.

Josh 2.0: Learning, Adapting, and Moving Forward

Josh's experiences have changed him. They have forced him to reevaluate his beliefs about work, leadership, and trust: made him cautious, aware of red flags, and discerning in the battles he chooses to fight. He no longer assumes that people are always working toward a shared goal, but he lives in hope. He has learned that some people operate entirely out of self-interest. Rather than allowing that realization to make him cynical, he uses it as a tool to understand people better, to navigate systems strategically, and to protect himself from unnecessary harm. While he has developed an ability to recognize narcissistic micromanagers from a distance, what still frustrates him is the collective silence encountered in so many organizations, the refusal to acknowledge problems that everyone can see.

"We all know what the elephant in the room is, so why are we still walking around it?"

As he looks for his next new role, Josh reflects on how to avoid carrying the bad experiences of the past into the next workplace and focusing on his many positive experiences.

Statistics: As reported by Ståhl, in a Flash Eurobarometer survey in 2022, The European Agency for Health and Safety at Work (EU-OSHA) found that 46% of respondents were subject to severe time pressure or overload of work. About a quarter (26%) referred to poor communication or co-operation within their organization and 18% to a lack of autonomy or influence over the pace of work or work processes. Violence or verbal abuse from customers or patients affected 16% of respondents and 7% reported harassment or bullying at work. In its latest report, the EU-OSHA also highlighted the link between workplace stress and heart disease.

Mary's Story: A Journey with Technical Hurdles

Mary's story is one of resilience, survival, and self-reclamation. On the surface, her childhood seemed stable—good education, strong family ties—but beneath it, fractures ran deep. Divorce, dysfunction, and the presence of a narcissistic parent shaped her earliest experiences. She learned quickly that the person who should have protected her was unreliable. She experienced periods of neglect, there were certainly moments where she was deprioritized, where she had to carry the emotional weight of others far too young.

The turning point came at a time when life should have been opening up, but instead, it closed in. A death in the family, another parental divorce, and an abusive home environment left Mary struggling with a period of anxiety and depression. It was a moment of reckoning: if no one else was going to take care of her, she would have to do it herself.

So she did!

Mary pursued college, earning multiple degrees, determined to create a life that was hers alone. Then, she left. She moved from Australia to the US, putting distance between herself and the past. It was a decade of hard work, of pushing through, of proving to herself that she was capable. But the body keeps score.

A back injury, sustained before she even left Australia, worsened before it became better, and in some ways was a metaphor for a lack of support Mary experienced during these critical years and her response to it under the relentless pressure she put on herself. The stress, the long hours, the constant need to prove her worth through hard work and achievement all culminated in an severe autoimmune disorder. It was a moment of reckoning, one that forced her to reevaluate everything. Her health, her outlook, and her body.

It was also the first time she experienced bullying in the workplace.

She had been driven by the desire to rebuild herself, but she hadn't yet learned how to protect herself from toxic environments. Mary's actions were always from a place of kindness and professionalism. She treated others with the respect that she would expect from herself. She still invested her energy in proving she belonged, finally realizing that some people would always seek to undermine her. Worse, they would use her kindness to undermine her. The stress of work and the mistreatment she endured directly coincided with flare-ups of her condition.

Amid all of this, she became a mother. A role she had longed for, one that grounded her, but added complexity. While supporting her husband through his studies, while navigating illness and recovery, she also had to rebuild her career after maternity leave. Deciding to return to Australia meant a return to the family dynamics she had left behind.

The Professional Battles That Followed

As she reentered the workforce, the same patterns followed. She was exceptionally talented in her field, in demand, constantly headhunted. It seemed though, that every company she landed in carried similar ethical issues, similar mistreatment, similar workplace politics, and similar inequities.

Sexism was omnipresent, woven into the very fabric of the industry she had chosen. Early in her career, she had realized that the way she dressed had an impact. She had toned down her femininity, subconsciously adapting to male-dominated environments. Even that wasn't enough.

One of her early interviewers, who later hired her, had admitted, after months of inappropriate flirtation, that he had only brought her on board because he was attracted to her. She had taken the job on the strength of her skills and experience, but in his mind, it was something else entirely. She endured it. She needed the job.

Then, she left.

The past always seems to have a way of catching up. The same man was hired by her next company (yes, the actual same man). She found herself in environments where she was objectified, dismissed, or excluded for simply having boundaries. For simply standing up for her personal dignity and self-respect.

She had fought so hard to be taken seriously, but time and again, she saw men coast into leadership roles while women had to fight for their place. She saw the "boys' club" in action, where promotions were secured not by merit but by social ties. As a single mum, she saw how exclusion worked in subtle ways—missed networking opportunities, being left out of conversations that happened at the pub, a lack of sponsorship because she wasn't visible in the spaces where deals were made.

Gaslighting, Burnout, and the Queen Bee Syndrome

The objectification of women was only one part of the problem. As her career progressed, she realized the real insidious issue was the way some women, especially those in leadership, perpetuated the very structures that held them back.

Mary encountered Queen Bee Syndrome: women in leadership positions who, rather than lifting other women up, sought to keep them down. Women who had fought tooth and nail to get where they were in male-dominated industries. One of Mary's network actively headhunted her for a leadership role, bringing her into a team that was being built. Instead of mentorship or support, Mary quickly realized she was an outsider in a tightly controlled hierarchy. There was an inner circle—the "favored bees"—and Mary wasn't in it despite consistently exceeding expectations and delivering results. Rather, she was asked to support the bees and build their capability but receive no rewards. When she shared an idea with her peers to seek their thoughts—an idea designed to improve workflow and collaboration—she was met with swift retaliation.

The message was clear: Stay in your lane. Don't overstep. Know your place. What struck Mary most was the hypocrisy. This leader spoke the language of heart-centered leadership, of collaboration, of bringing people along for the journey. When it came down to it, the tone was rigid, territorial, and ruled by ego. From that incident, the attempts to publicly humiliate Mary became frequent.

This was one of many learning experiences.

> **Definition: Gaslighting** is a psychological manipulation technique in which a person tries to convince someone that their reality is untrue.

In her next role, she was handed a high-profile project riddled with internal politics but without the support or scaffolding to succeed. The team and culture were fragmented, yet she was expected to bring cohesion. She raised concerns, pointed out the issues, but instead of being heard, she was gaslighted and excluded.

"I'd say something had happened. That I had evidence. Repeatedly. I was told, 'Oh no, it's not.'" She wasn't even met with an acknowledgment of her experience. No discussion, no disagreement—simply a flat-out denial. Leadership told her she was doing a fantastic job, all the way up until they served her with a redundancy package. The exit package. The nondisclosure agreement.

It was all so predictable.

She had been set up to fail.

Reclaiming Power

Through it all, Mary never stopped evolving. Therapy, self-reflection, and experience gave her the tools to navigate the workplace differently. She became strategic about where she invested her time and energy. She set boundaries. She let go of perfectionism.

She learned how to improve her health and life outlook through evolving practices, such as exercise, diet, self-care, and compassion. She now models the leadership she wants to see, even in environments that don't align with her values.

Now, she is conscious of where her energy is directed.

She knows that being a woman in leadership means moving through a world that isn't built for her success. She has seen the scarcity mindset play out—the way women are sometimes pitted against one another instead of lifting each other up.

She has also learned that there is space for everyone.

Mary has worked with incredible leaders: ones who definitely embodied heart-centered leadership. Leaders who were transparent, communicative, confident, but kind. Leaders who understood that leadership isn't about control—it's about trust.

While those leaders were rare, they proved that good leadership is possible.

Mary knows that leadership cannot continue in its current form and believes that the future is about relationships, about recognizing humanity in the workplace. For Mary, leadership is about creating workplaces where people are set up to succeed, and most importantly, it is about recognizing that no one should have to endure what she endured to build a successful career.

She is still in demand. Still sought after.

This time, she is the one doing the choosing.

4

The Moments That Make a Difference

The Leadership Confidence Trap

I know what it's like to sit at a table and feel like you don't belong. To question whether you deserve the seat. To wonder if you're about to be found out—as if somehow you've tricked people into believing you're capable, when deep down, you're convinced you're not. That's *imposter syndrome*, and for most of my career in male-dominated workplaces, I carried it with me. That inner voice—the one that doubts your abilities, downplays your achievements, and whispers that you don't deserve success—was with me everywhere. Every presentation and every leadership role. It wasn't simply the workplace dynamics that fueled it. Growing up with a parent like mine, I learned that my achievements were not my own; they were credited to someone else, or worse, minimized to keep me in my place. I internalized the belief that no matter what I accomplished, essentially it was never *mine*.

> **Definition: Imposter syndrome** is the persistent inability to believe that your success is deserved or has been legitimately achieved.

When I walked into corporate spaces where men took credit for my work, where my voice wasn't welcomed, and where I was actively excluded, I wasn't simply battling workplace sexism. I was battling years of conditioning that told me I wasn't enough.

One experience stands out as both a defining challenge and a breakthrough moment. At the time, I was leading a huge cost-reduction program for a well-known Australian corporate organization. A major part of my role was to report quarterly to a board subcommittee, chaired by a man who made his views painfully clear: women were not welcome at the table. If we had to be there, we were to remain silent. Every meeting was a minefield.

I prepared meticulously, but I wasn't allowed to present my own work. My manager delivered my presentations as if they were his. When board members asked questions, he answered in ways I wouldn't have and not necessarily with the full picture, leaving me helpless. With each meeting, my self-doubt grew.

Maybe I wasn't supposed to speak.

Maybe I wasn't capable.

Maybe I really didn't belong.

Then, everything shifted. During a meeting with many important decisions on the table, one of the subcommittee members asked a detailed financial question, a question that required an answer based on intricate knowledge of the data and its analysis. My manager sat in awkward silence, unable to respond. A few of the open-minded subcommittee members turned to me. "Do you know the answer?" I had a choice: stay silent and reinforce the belief that I didn't belong, or speak up and prove—if only to myself—that I did.

I chose to speak.

I explained the analysis, clarified the numbers, and addressed their concerns—calmly, confidently, and with complete authority. In that moment, I realized that the only person doubting my abilities in that room was me.

I knew my work. I deserved my seat. And I was fully capable of leading the conversation. Inevitably there were consequences; the leadership culture and the dominant male environment in that organization weren't ready for my personal revelation. I was no longer invited to attend those meetings. The message was clear: Women who challenge the status quo (i.e., speak in public) don't get a seat at the table. At first, the exclusion stung, but then, something shifted.

I understood that my value wasn't dictated by whether others recognized it—it was dictated by whether I did.

Imposter syndrome doesn't disappear overnight, but I've learned it can be managed, challenged, and rewritten. Here's what helped me—and what I now pass on to others for them to help manage their own imposter syndrome.

Name It and Call It Out

If you don't acknowledge imposter syndrome, it stays in the shadows and controls you. It's not a reflection of your actual ability; it's a distorted story your self-doubt is telling you. According to *Forbes* magazine, about 78 percent of business leaders report experiencing imposter syndrome at some point. If you're feeling it, you're not alone—and it's not the truth.

→ *Next time you doubt yourself, say this out loud:* "I feel like I don't belong, but that feeling doesn't mean it's true. I am capable. I have earned my place. I belong."

Fight feelings with facts when imposter syndrome creeps in. Pull out those memories that give you the hard evidence of your accomplishments.

- Keep a file of positive feedback and comments.
- Write down times your work made a difference to the organization and its people.
- List moments when you stepped up and delivered. Give yourself extra credit if you pushed through fear.

You didn't get lucky. You earned it.

Talk About It (Because You Are Not Alone)

The moment I started opening up about my doubts, I realized that even the most successful people I admired had felt the same way. By sharing, we normalize the experience and remind ourselves that doubt is part of growth—not proof of incompetence.

- Find mentors, trusted colleagues, or friends to talk to, people who can help you challenge that pesky voice of the inner critic.

Reframe Failure as Growth

Heart-centered leadership is about creating and existing in an environment of psychological safety—that means for you too! I've learned to treat my own mistakes the way I would treat a struggling team member—with compassion, not judgment. Remember that mistakes are lessons, setbacks are data points, and progress matters more than perfection. As someone recovering from chronic perfectionism, I've come to embrace the idea that being effective is far more important than being flawless. I've learned to be kind to myself and celebrate my humanity.

Celebrate Every Win—Even the Small Ones

Take a moment to acknowledge your achievements: not only the big career-defining successes, but the small daily victories that generally take as much mental energy.

- Speaking up in a meeting when you felt nervous.
- Owning an achievement without downplaying it.
- Pushing through self-doubt and doing it anyway.

Every time you challenge imposter syndrome, you weaken its hold on you.

You belong.

You are capable.

You have earned your place.

You are not an imposter.

That voice of self-doubt may never fully go away—but you can learn to turn down the volume and drown it out with truth. Your perspective, your voice, and your leadership are needed. The moments that feel the most uncomfortable are the moments when you're growing into the leader you were always meant to be.

Figure 8: Curious me with my granddad

Figure 9: My dad in our backyard in 1967

> "They do everything to dim your light, and then they ask you why you're not shining."
>
> —Najwa Zebian, activist, author, poet, educator, and speaker

> "There are a million cheap seats in the world today filled with people who will never be brave with their own lives but will spend every ounce of energy they have hurling advice and judgement at those of us trying to dare greatly. Their only contributions are criticism, cynicism, and fearmongering."
>
> —Brené Brown, author of *Dare to Lead*

> "Yesterday I was clever, so I wanted to change the world; today I am wise, so I am changing myself."
>
> —Rumi, 13th-century poet and Islamic scholar

"Humans have a fundamental need to belong. Just as we have needs for food and water, we also have needs for positive and lasting relationships. This need is deeply rooted in our evolutionary history."

—Dr. C. Nathan DeWall, psychology professor

Figure 10: My granddad

My Defining Moment: Leaving Trauma and Toxicity Behind

Well, here it is: the tough bit to write. The part where I demonstrate my vulnerability.

Imposter syndrome doesn't exist in a vacuum. It feeds off the environments we find ourselves in. For years, I questioned myself—*Was I good enough? Did I deserve my success? Was I truly capable? Was I fooling everyone around me?* What I hadn't fully realized was that self-doubt thrives in toxic spaces. It magnifies in environments that gaslight, undermine, and manipulate. When you grow up learning to make yourself invisible in order to survive, as I did, those patterns don't disappear when you step into leadership. They manifest in new ways.

For me, my greatest defining moment—the moment that shattered my self-doubt and rewrote my story—came when I faced the most dysfunctional leadership culture of my career. It was there I finally understood why I struggled for so long—and why I needed to break free. It was through this struggle I truly understood the transformative potential of leading from the heart.

Many years ago, I started a role that, on paper, was perfect. It combined my personal values with my professional goals in business optimization, something I had been looking for. The organization, although still corporate in nature, delivered a product that resonated with my values. A role that my granddad would have been proud of; I felt that by taking this job, I was honouring his legacy and the countless hours he spent encouraging me to dream bigger and aim higher.

I walked in full of optimism. Then, reality hit. The red flags of a destructive culture started immediately. Upon meeting a peer for the first time, he greeted me: "You were hired because this place needs leadership." It wasn't a compliment. It was a warning. The deeper I looked, the more dysfunction I found. Despite a profitable product, there were no clear accountabilities and the strategic goals that did exist were vague. Decisions were made to protect egos, not to improve the organization or serve its customer base. The organization was pursuing growth into other customer segments, but it lacked the foundational infrastructure to support expansion. And at the center of it all?

My boss.

He was relentless, piling on tasks without context, micromanaging everything, demanding rework, while making it impossible to succeed. The worst part was that I found myself slipping into old patterns: I doubted my instincts. I questioned my expertise, and I wondered if I was the problem. That is exactly how toxic leaders keep people in their place.

The truth hit me in a huge *aha!* moment: he was twisting situations, exploiting my need to prove myself in a new job, reacting with offense when I asked questions—as if my curiosity were a personal attack. He constantly needed validation, became petty and jealous when I connected with mutual stakeholders, and played the victim card to manipulate me.

I realized: He was exactly like my dad. He was a *narcissist!*

My initial reaction was panic. How had I got myself into the laser-sights of a narcissist again? Had he chosen to hire me because I was easy to manipulate and not because of my skills?

He surrounded himself with sycophants—fellow males who prioritized managing his image over the operations and customers. These people weren't there to lead; they were there to protect him and his position. Together they worked to undermine others by weaponizing information. They fed his paranoia while ignoring real concerns, and they created a culture of secrecy and manipulation. It didn't matter how hard I worked; I would never be accepted in this space.

Despite the way I was treated, my team thrived. Under my leadership, they brought their expertise to the forefront, excelled in their roles, and validated what I knew deep down: I was a good leader. Their success made me realize the questions I was asking about organizational efficiency were valid and my contributions significant. That success is exactly what made me a threat.

The more effective my team became, the more my boss sought to undermine me. Any strategy I proposed was dismissed, critical information was withheld, and I was even accused of "catastrophizing" when I spoke the truth about the lack of infrastructure to expand the product.

The moment I realized I was once again in the wrong room was when one of the sycophants with no process improvement experience challenged my expertise, calling me unreasonable. My boss sided with him without seeking first to understand the basics. They won the battle, and I lost something bigger. I lost my sense of safety. From that moment, I knew I wasn't safe to share my expertise, to lead with my own values, or to bring my best self to work. Every idea I put forward was dismantled, criticized, or erased—even when the organization itself was thanking me for my work. This experience triggered something deeper.

The old wounds from my childhood resurfaced: life was repeating itself. I was walking on those eggshells I had learned to navigate, trying to survive someone else's unpredictable emotions. Buried childhood traumas were brought to the surface; some I had long been aware of, others I had unknowingly suppressed.

At my lowest point one night, I called a suicide prevention hotline. The stress, the gaslighting, the manipulation, the relentless attacks on my self-worth, made me feel like I couldn't breathe. My anxiety skyrocketed, and I experienced physical symptoms that made it clear my body was bearing the brunt of the stress. I cried in isolation daily, struggled with insomnia, questioned my sanity, and felt like I was barely holding on.

I needed help.

Then came another turning point: a retreat, and a therapist who changed my life. At a meditation retreat in the hills over a gloriously sunny long weekend, I met a therapist who listened to my story. She softly uttered one word that reframed my entire existence. *Abuse.*

No one had ever described my experiences using that word before. Not in forty plus years. That's what it was—abuse! What I endured as a child and what I was enduring now. For the first time in my life, I saw the full picture. What a moment of clarity!

This wasn't about a bad boss.

This wasn't about workplace politics.

This wasn't about me struggling to cope.

This was a system designed to keep people like me—strong, competent, and empathic—in the shadows.

For years, I convinced myself my dad wasn't so bad. Perhaps I had exaggerated my experiences. In the same way, in this workplace, I kept telling myself my boss couldn't possibly be as destructive as he seemed. My fundamental belief that people are inherently good had led me into a situation that eroded my sense of self-worth.

I was done playing that game.

However, instead of moving on, I clung onto the opportunity to fill in for his position while he took parental leave, a role that would allow me to expand my expertise. I saw this as a gift. Little did I know that the gift was actually a curse. As I prepared to take this on, my boss withheld critical information, forcing me to fight for the knowledge I needed to succeed during his absence. His derisive attitude and secret conversations between him and his sycophants became hurdles. Behind the scenes, he sowed discord, instructing others to bypass my authority. To fuel my imposter syndrome, he planted doubt among my team, telling them I lacked the necessary skills to succeed, telling them he was afraid of the "mess" I would leave in my wake. In one final act of sabotage, my manager apologized to the Head of Finance (a peer), another ego-driven manager, that he wasn't given the opportunity to fill in for the parental leave. The consequence? One narcissist stepped aside temporarily, another emboldened by this apology, stepped forward.

The Head of Finance refused to collaborate with me, dangerously failed to fulfill his financial responsibilities, and even lodged an official complaint with the CEO when I held him accountable for his deliverables and for the way he treated people. His actions were a constant source of frustration, but I knew I faced a systemic issue created by toxic culture.

During this time, I leaned heavily on the support of my therapist, who helped me see this period not as the punishment it felt like but as a healing opportunity. The challenges of dealing with command-and-control leadership, echoing my dad's treatment of me as a child, became a gift. They forced me to confront and heal from the deeply ingrained fears and doubts that I had carried for years. This wasn't about surviving a toxic workplace; it was about finally breaking free from the emotional chains of my past.

I had met a monster that was worse than all those that came before.

The senior role tested me in ways I never imagined. Yet, it also gave me moments of triumph. I navigated meetings with poise, earned praise from peers, and found allies. My team's unwavering support and the gratitude of others fueled my resolve to lead with heart-centred values. By the end of my time, I had survived and proved to myself I could take on a wider range of responsibilities. The acknowledgement from my team and the wider organization was deeply humbling, a powerful affirmation that my leadership style, combined with my innate abilities, was my greatest strength. I realized I had been listening to critics all my life; this time I started listening to the gratitude and the praise.

Then he came back.

Upon his return, his hostility reached new heights. My success shattered his narrative of my incompetence, and his insecurities translated into open aggression. He ignored my contributions and began systematically undoing everything I had achieved. My initiatives to improve customer retention were dismantled, and I was accused of causing the staff to feel uncomfortable despite the fact I championed staff well-being. What a cruel distortion of my greatest strength. The environment became unbearable as my colleagues, influenced by his rhetoric, began treating me differently. I endured months of being ignored, undermined, and criticized. Yet, something within me had changed.

I had faced my monster and emerged stronger.

I began calling out the game-playing and challenging the dynamics. I set boundaries, refused to participate in manipulative tactics, and stood firm in my values. Despite the cracks starting to show under the relentless pressure, I continued to lead my team and improve efficiency with the same heart-centred approach, knowing it was the only way to stay true to myself. It was my passion.

Leaving that organization was actually a very difficult decision, I walked away with activities unfinished, growth into new sectors in infancy, with customers satisfaction still needing improvement—but I walked away stronger than ever. Because now, I knew the truth. The truth was I had never been the problem. I had always been enough, and I promised myself that I was finally done living in spaces that tried to convince me otherwise.

Forbes magazine talks about a concept called *post-traumatic growth*—the positive transformation that happens after surviving something devastating. I certainly experienced this phenomenon, but I renamed it as *finally stepping into who I was meant to be.*

This experience didn't break me. It built me.

It's the reason I am here today, sharing this story, and proving that heart-centered leadership is powerful and necessary to ensure fear-based bullying leadership retires and is left to the past with my Industrial Revolution ancestors from Angel Meadows.

Statistics: Gallup's World Risk Poll 2021: Safe at Work? Global experiences of violence and harassment key findings:

- Among people who have worked at some point in their lifetime, one in five reported experiencing some form of violence and harassment at work in their lifetime (20.9%).
  - ▷ *Of those who reported experience of violence and harassment, more than half experienced it more than once (58.5%).*
- Men were slightly more likely than women to report experience of violence and harassment at work (21.9% vs 19.8%).
- Psychological violence and harassment was the most frequently reported form (16.5%) compared to physical (7.4%) and sexual (5.5%).
  - ▷ *Of those who reported experiencing violence and harassment at work, over a quarter of people reported experiencing multiple forms of it (27.7%).*
  - ▷ *For a third of women who reported experiencing any violence and harassment, there was a sexual element to this experience (32.9%). This dropped to one in six for men (15.4%).*
- Australia and New Zealand reported the highest levels of experience, at nearly one in two people (47.9%).
- In this and other Western regions, there was a significant gap between the sexes, with women much more likely to say they had experienced violence and harassment at work than men.

Leading When Life Falls Apart

Toxic leadership doesn't only test you; it forces you to confront what kind of leader you really are and discover your capacity for resilience. For me, surviving in a dysfunctional leadership environment was about getting through the day with some sanity while finding a way to lead and protect my team from the toxicity. Tough times demand clarity, compassion, and a steadfast commitment to principles, qualities that have held me in good stead.

At the same time I was navigating the fallout from my manager's return, I was leading a major organizational improvement initiative, where I was needed as a stabilizing force. Tension and uncertainty were weighing heavily over the entire workforce. Some people worried about their job security while others struggled to adapt to new ways of working. Through it all, my boss wasted no time reestablishing his control and actively working against me. His hostility and gamesmanship escalated. He openly dismissed my process improvement expertise and tried to erase my contributions, clearly placing his ego above the needs of the organization. I had a choice: let the chaos consume me or stay steady for my team, the organization, and the customers we were trying to service.

I chose to stay steady.

Leadership isn't only about what you do in easy times; it's about how you show up when everything is falling apart.

In the middle of all of it, I needed to return to the UK because I lost a very dear cousin, placing me in a position of having to face the shadow of another demon—my dad. My dad returned to England many years earlier, and we hadn't spoken since, a silence borne from decades of unresolved issues. Being in the same country as him, with the fear of having to face him, brought a flood of unresolved emotions: anger for the way he shaped my childhood through fear, sadness for the things we would never have the courage to say to each other. I didn't have the strength to see him, given the parallel experiences at work. So I found myself on a plane to the UK, worried about facing a man who cast such a long and complicated shadow over my life. All the while, I was worried because I knew that game-playing to unsettle me was continuing at work. I managed to avoid my dad that trip, but not the heavy knots of an anxious stomach. When I got back, I felt like I returned to a war zone. My boss's campaign against me had escalated, and now the sycophants were weighing in more heavily.

Despite the emotional weight, I threw myself into my work upon my return. My team needed me, and I needed the focus. I focused on what I could control: leading with vulnerability and empathy, listening to people, and most importantly, creating a sense of stability for my team, even when I had none myself. I poured my energy into one of my passions, embedding LEAN principles, one of the only things that gave me purpose at the time and something the organization desperately needed. That project became my lifeline and a way to channel my energy. It reminded me of why I loved leading through complex challenges, why I was good at what I did, and why I deserved to be there, despite best efforts to make me feel otherwise.

Looking back, that period was one of the hardest in my career, but it also taught me or reaffirmed some important leadership lessons.

- Leadership isn't about pretending to be strong; it's about showing up, even when you feel broken, and doing what needs to be done when people rely on you.
- Vulnerability isn't a weakness; it's what allows you to lean into genuineness.
- Holding fast to your personal values and principles will guide you through the darkest moments.

Even as I faced my demons from my past, and my credibility was challenged at work, I refused to lose myself in the chaos.

That's how I knew I had already won.

Being Relatable: The Power of Vulnerability

Another truth I've learned about leadership is that it's not about being untouchable; it's about being human.

Genuineness is what connects us, and in leadership, it's what builds trust, inspires teams, and creates real belonging.

The moment I embraced my own insecurities, I became a better leader. This was reinforced with the recent loss of my dad. He passed away, with us never having spoken, never having said those unsaid things. I made another trek back to the UK to reunite with family members, together saying goodbye at his funeral. That chapter closed, and I was ready to return to Australia to start a new chapter.

I learned the power of vulnerability when I shared the loss of my dad with my team. I didn't pretend I was fine. I didn't shove down the grief and put on a performance. I let myself be vulnerable, and I became relatable. Being relatable allowed me to bridge the gap between authority and humanity, reminding people that everybody, even those in leadership, face challenges. It deepened my connection with my team. They saw me not only as a leader but as a person. But not every leadership environment allows vulnerability. I learned that the hard way from a boss who saw me as a machine and not a human.

Years earlier, I had worked as a contractor, reporting to a boss who represented everything I wanted to avoid becoming as a leader. rigid, dismissive, and utterly unsupportive. He was far more concerned with control than compassion. At the time, I was already stretched thin, juggling the financial pressures of single parenthood and the relentless demands of work.

One night, I had to make an incredibly difficult phone call. My brother had taken his own life, and I needed to fly to Tasmania to be with my grief-stricken mum and dad. When I told my boss during that challenging call, his reaction left me stunned. No condolences. No concern. Just cold indifference. He only cared about the meetings I would miss. Five days later, while I was still with my family in Tasmania, he called me but not to ask how I was and not to check if I was OK. To demand that I return to work immediately or risk losing my job. I had no choice; I needed to pay bills and keep a roof over our heads. I packed up my grief, dragged my daughter back home and back to school far too soon, and returned to work as if nothing happened.

When I walked into the office, I discovered that the meetings I had been rushed back for were manufactured. They weren't urgent. They could have been postponed. I was furious. He hadn't even told my colleagues what happened, leaving me to explain my absence. Facing their kindness (which was lovely) only made me more emotional. Then, he made one final, gut-wrenching comment to my face over a cup of coffee: "Suicide is a sin."

The judgment.

The lack of compassion.

The complete dehumanization of what I was going through. I will never forget it. That experience broke something in me but not in the way he intended; it made me even more determined to lead differently. It solidified my commitment to being a leader who listens, who creates safe spaces, and who values *people*, not as workers nor as corporate cogs. I resolved that no one under my leadership would feel unsupported or silenced in their time of need.

I vowed that one day, I would create workplaces where no one would ever feel like I did in that moment.

What Kind of Leader Will You Choose to Be?

Every leader will face catastrophe, loss, and moments that test them. The real question is "who do you choose to be in those moments?"

Do you lead with control, indifference, and fear?

Or do you lead with empathy, integrity, and heart?

In every one of my defining moments, I have been tested, and every time I chose to lead with my heart. I might have lost sight of myself, but I never lost sight of who I was as a leader. In my world, that is the definition of leadership.

> "There are no templates or prescriptions for recovering our health and well-being. Recovery occurs through connection, attunement, care, humility... and a few skills."
>
> —Anne Ligthart, psychotherapist

> "A leader is a dealer in hope."
>
> —Napoleon Bonaparte, French general and statesman

THE MOMENTS THAT MAKE A DIFFERENCE

Figure 11: Me at primary school in a cardigan knitted by my mum

"A little consideration, a little thought for others, makes all the difference."

—Eeyore, *Winnie-the-Pooh*, by A. A. Milne

Eve's Story: A Geek's Journey to Leadership

I reached out to Eve to talk about leadership, only to discover that her passion for leadership theory is deeply rooted in her own lived experience. Her journey, shaped by a challenging childhood and career highs and lows, ultimately led her to study and apply leadership in a way that blends intellectual curiosity with real-world lessons.

A Different Kind of Childhood

Eve describes herself as "quite an imaginative kid, a bit left of center," a trait amplified by an unstable home life. Her mother, a scientist, was pragmatic and distant, while her father worked two jobs, leading to financial stress and volatility. "I didn't really know how to be with people. I wasn't comfortable at home, and I wasn't comfortable at school either."

Her differences made her a target for bullying, but in high school, she found her voice and a group of friends who made her feel less alone. Still, she kept parts of her life hidden. "I never brought friends home—I was worried about how my dad would behave."

A turning point came when her father suffered a heart attack when she was in tenth grade, transforming him overnight into a calm, present parent. Later, during university, she learned of her mother's struggles with workplace illness. A laboratory failure to install proper filtering equipment had left multiple employees, including her mother, severely ill. Her work cover claims were denied, and she was gaslighted into believing nothing was wrong. "It showed me how those in power could ignore the suffering of others."

These experiences cemented Eve's belief in advocacy. "How do I find my voice? How do I advocate for others? My sister and I both went into careers where we could fight for people who, like our mother, weren't heard."

From University to Leadership Lessons

Eve's early career included roles that ranged from frustrating to formative. She entered university administration, believing she could drive change but quickly realized she was an outsider in a rigid system. Eventually, she landed a role at another university, where she encountered both the best and worst leaders of her career.

Her first great leader took her under his wing. "He let me shadow him, brought me to every meeting, and explained his decisions. He trusted me with big responsibilities." Another influential leader, later her long-term boss, led with humility and care. "He had no ego. He once told me, 'You'll never break anything so much that we can't fix it.'" What set these leaders apart was simple—they gave her their time.

The shift came when a new leader took over. "At first, she saw me as a strong operator, but I wasn't a 'yes' person. When I questioned things, the relationship soured." Eve learned firsthand about in-groups and out-groups when the new boss hired people from her previous workplace, creating a divide between those who agreed with her and those who didn't. "I was always willing to support a decision once it was made, but I wasn't in the in-group anymore."

Her next leader had different strengths but also resisted being challenged. "She believed she was empowering, but really she wanted people to agree with her. There's a big difference between someone who is command-and-control and knows it and someone who is command-and-control but thinks they're a collaborative leader. That difference is emotional intelligence."

For Eve, these experiences fueled her lifelong focus: "How do you show up? How do you call things out? How do you constructively dissent? That will be my life's work."

Geeking Out on Leadership

Eve's leadership studies have led her to explore "followership"—the idea that leadership isn't only about the leader, but about how people choose to follow. "A command-and-control leader has followership, but it's through fear. A transformational or servant leader has followership because they invest in relationships and share power."

She frequently references Leader-Member Exchange (LMX) Theory, which explores in-groups and out-groups. "Great leaders build large in-groups. Once you're in an out-group, regaining influence is nearly impossible—you usually have to wait for a leadership change." Her personal experiences reinforced this. "When I was suddenly on the receiving end of my manager's attitude shift, I wasn't doing my job any differently—I wasn't in her in-group anymore."

Another major lesson came from watching leaders struggle with empowerment. "Many people talk about creating 'authorizing environments' but don't truly understand it. As a leader, you have to trust others to do the work, and if they fail, you're accountable. If you can't handle that, you shouldn't be in the role." This took her back to the advice of her great leader: "You'll never break anything so much that we can't fix it."

She also explores the balance leaders must strike. "How do you stay close enough to the work to ensure it's done well, but give people the autonomy to innovate? Many leaders struggle to transition from being an expert to leading through others."

Situational Leadership in Action

After returning from maternity leave, Eve inherited what she calls "the worst team I've ever seen." They lacked commitment, were unkind to each other, and dismissed her authority. "They didn't care about the work or the business. Some were outright disrespectful."

She turned to situational leadership—a model that tailors leadership style to an employee's experience and ability. However, she realized too late that she had misjudged the situation. "I think what I failed to do in this situation was recognize that I had a team of people who thought they were expert in the work. The real challenge was that they didn't recognize their own lack of expertise." For Eve, this was a key lesson. "Situational leadership is never a fixed point in time."

She also learned about her own leadership style. "I have some laissez-faire traits—not in a way that I don't care, but I focus on outcomes over process. A colleague suggested I'd be better suited to managing senior people, and it made me think. I prefer strategy over micromanagement."

One of her proudest moments came from leading outside her expertise. "A data infrastructure manager I led—despite knowing nothing about his field—once told me I was the best leader he'd ever had. Our conversations weren't technical; they were about what he needed to succeed." This reinforced for her that real leadership is about enabling others, removing roadblocks, and trusting people to do their jobs.

The Future of Leadership

Eve is a little skeptical about how leadership theories are taught and applied. "What I think leadership theories do, is help a person reflect on their own approach to the way that they show up." She doesn't believe simply teaching theories makes a difference unless people reflect on their success at applying them. "Great leaders are great learners. If you reflect and think at the end of each week, then you are going to be better at whatever it is you do."

"Empathetic leadership is the way forward. In the future, technology will handle tasks we can't even imagine today. Technical skills will become less relevant—emotional intelligence will be key." Younger generations expect flexibility and personalization in work. "Future leaders will need to build relationships and lead through change."

However, she acknowledges the tension between emotional intelligence and stability. "In uncertain times, people crave certainty. That leads to command-and-control structures, as people want someone to remove the mental load."

As a final thought, Eve introduced an emerging theory, "Systems Leadership," a theory that examines entire work environments to improve outcomes for everyone. "It's about looking at the whole system of work to make work better for all people."

In the final chapter where I contemplate the future of leadership, we'll explore the influential intersection between systems leadership and heart-centered leadership, examining how leading with both a systemic mindset and emotional intelligence creates workplaces where people thrive, innovation flourishes, and long-term success becomes possible.

Your Turn to Geek Out on Leadership Theories

If you want to learn about the theories Eve mentioned, here are some short descriptions.

Constructive Dissent: The Catalyst for Innovation and Growth
Ever been in a meeting where everyone nods in agreement, even when you know there are better ideas left unspoken? That's where constructive dissent comes into play. *Cutting Edge PR* describes it as the practice of encouraging open, respectful debate within the workplace, allowing team members to voice differing opinions without fear. This kind of environment doesn't merely tolerate alternative viewpoints—it embraces them as pathways to growth and innovation.

When leaders normalize dissent, they create a culture where questioning the existing state of affairs is expected. This approach leads to better decision-making, as it considers a wider array of perspectives and potential solutions. Add in psychological safety and people feel secure in expressing their thoughts, knowing they won't face negative repercussions. By focusing on ideas rather than individuals, teams can engage in productive discussions that challenge assumptions and lead to better outcomes.

Followership: The Other Side of Leadership
Great leadership doesn't exist without great followership. It's not about being passive, blindly following orders, or sitting back while someone else takes charge. True followership is active, engaged, and essential to any successful organization.

Think about it—leaders set the vision, but it's the followers who bring that vision to life. Remember the *"Do as I say!"* executive from chapter one? According to a blog by Bethel University, strong followers think critically, ask questions, challenge ideas when necessary, and contribute to solutions rather than waiting for instructions. The best teams succeed because everyone plays a role in driving things forward. It's not about hierarchy—it's about a partnership. Heart-centered leaders are naturally inclined to embrace partnerships. The best leaders create space for strong followership, and the best followers make leaders better. It's a two-way street, and when done right it makes teams unstoppable.

Laissez-Faire Leadership: When Leaders Step Back
Imagine a workplace where the boss says, "You've got this," and then steps aside, trusting you and giving you the freedom to tackle projects your way. That's the essence of laissez-faire leadership according to *Very Well Mind*. It's a hands-off approach where leaders provide minimal direction and allow team members to make decisions. This style works wonders when you have a team of highly skilled, self-motivated individuals who thrive on independence. However, without clear guidance, it can lead to confusion and a dip in productivity. So, while it offers autonomy, it requires a team that's ready to handle responsibility.

**Leader-Member Exchange (LMX) Theory:
The Dynamics of Workplace Relationships**
Ever noticed how some employees share a close rapport with their managers, while others maintain a strictly professional distance? Leader-Member Exchange (LMX) Theory examines these dynamics, highlighting that leaders naturally form varying relationships with team members. The *Decision Lab* clearly describes in-group and out-group behavior as experienced by Eve. Those in the "in-group" enjoy higher trust, more responsibilities, and greater access to resources, leading to increased job satisfaction and performance. Conversely, "out-group" members may experience a more formal relationship, sticking closely to their job descriptions without additional perks.

Situational Leadership: Adapting Your Style to Fit the Team

Ever noticed how some leaders seem to have a knack for adjusting their approach based on the situation at hand? That's the essence of Situational Leadership—the idea that there's no one-size-fits-all method to leading effectively. *Very Well Mind* describes great leaders as assessing their team's readiness and competence, then tailoring their leadership style accordingly. For instance, when guiding a novice team member, a leader might take a directive approach, providing clear instructions and close supervision. Conversely, with seasoned professionals, a leader can adopt a delegative style, while remaining available for support. This flexibility ensures that leadership is responsive to the unique demands of each situation, fostering an environment where both leaders and their teams thrive.

Systems Leadership: Navigating Complexity with Heart

Systems Leadership is a holistic approach that recognizes leadership as a collective process rather than the actions of one individual at the top. At its core, Systems Leadership (defined by the *World Economic Forum*) is about understanding the complex, interconnected nature of organizations. It acknowledges that no leader operates in isolation—every decision, action, and interaction are part of a broader system.

Unlike traditional leadership models that focus on top-down authority, Systems Leadership understands that real change happens when leadership is distributed, and people at all levels feel empowered to contribute. It's about shifting from control to connection, from hierarchy to networks, and from individual success to collective impact (*Villar's Institute*).

5

My Inner Transformation

From Survival Mode to Heart Mode: My Self-Empowerment

> **Definition: Self-empowerment** is claiming control over your own life. It's about making intentional choices, taking decisive action, and trusting in your ability to shape your future. At its core, it's about nurturing an unshakable sense of self-worth and confidence, knowing you are capable and deserving of the life you want.

Personal growth and professional achievement are intertwined when it comes to journeying through leadership. My approach to leading from the heart wasn't built in boardrooms or management textbooks, it was forged through my lived experiences and some of the most painful and defining moments of my life.

It **started** with loss—the death of my brother, the struggles of single parenthood, and the weight of imposter syndrome.

Then, it became clear in the toxic environments that mirrored my childhood, forcing me to confront long-buried wounds.

Finally, it fully took shape when I was crucified for being a good leader.

I lived through the fire that shaped my leadership style and my personal philosophy. When I came out the other side, I had yet another *aha!* moment: heart-centered leadership was a way of leading for me, but it was also my survival.

For years, I carried the weight of imposter syndrome.

I questioned my instincts.

I played small.

I told myself the problem was me.

I had spent a lifetime trying to earn my place at the table, both at home and at work. The reality was I had been strong, capable, and worthy all along. Every time I faced a bully the experience got worse, then when toxicity finally tried to break me, it did the opposite; it set me free. I look back now and thank those many dysfunctional leaders for their gift, the gift of forcing me to confront my deepest wounds and face my fears. The gift to rewire my self-worth with clarity: not only transforming my career, but transforming me. I finally saw the cycles I had been trapped in. I chose to reclaim my voice.

It became the culmination of my journey to heal from narcissistic abuse.

I've learned many things along the way. However, my *key* lessons, the basic building blocks of my transformation, are summarized by the following.

Resilience Isn't About Endurance—It's About Healing

People love to call me "resilient." "You've survived so much. You're so strong." But resilience isn't about surviving hardship—it comes from reflecting and healing from the pain. Confronting the unhealthy dynamics that I faced, forced me to recognize recurring patterns from my past. Patterns I had unknowingly carried into my personal and professional life. Through therapy and self-reflection, I realized that breaking free from these cycles required more than survival; it required reframing challenges as opportunities to redefine my leadership and my sense of self-worth. Resilience is about stepping into your power, even when circumstances push you to question it. Kathryn McEwen from *Working with Resilience* eloquently describes it: "Resilience is a life-long journey. None of us can claim it as a permanent state."

Empathy Is the Antidote to Toxicity

Fear-based leadership thrives in combative environments where people feel unseen, unheard, and unsafe. My journey showed me that empathy, listening, understanding, and valuing the experiences of others—can counteract even the most vile work cultures. I gave myself permission to make some choices.

I remained genuine to my values.

I created spaces where people felt seen and valued.

I built trust where others built fear.

It worked. My teams flourished in the environment of psychological safety. They brought their best and new ideas to the table, meaning that collaboration, creativity, and trust became our natural team culture. What I didn't expect was that the more I made my teams happy to come to work, the more people outside my team gravitated toward us. They craved the safety and leadership that saw them as human. This is a lesson I continue to reflect on: how to balance empathy with sustainability, ensuring that it doesn't come at the cost of the leader's well-being.

Genuineness Is Your Superpower

For years, I believed if I were open about my struggles, the truth would be used against me. Growing up, I was conditioned to hide the challenges within my family, and as a single parent, I never let my struggles show. Pretending to have it all together actually doesn't make you a great leader. Being real does. Being genuine opened the door to meaningful connections that allowed my teams to lean on each other without feeling like a "family." We weren't a family—we were a group of respectful, supportive individuals. Contrary to articles warning against creating family-like dynamics in teams, I believe I found the right balance of connection and professionalism.

Boundaries Are Not Optional

In toxic environments, power and information are used as weapons:

- People who lack boundaries get steamrolled.
- People who set boundaries are seen as "difficult."

Boundaries are not about being difficult; they are about self-respect and sustainability. Setting boundaries protected my mental health and modeled healthy businesslike relationships for people I led. One moment stands out vividly: during a meeting with one of my managers, I firmly said, "This is game-playing, and I'm not playing anymore. It stops here." That simple statement shifted the entire conversation. Boundaries are not about confrontation: they are about clarity, strength, and integrity.

Courage Means Speaking Truth to Power

Calling out toxic leadership is terrifying, especially in cultures where dissent is punished. However, staying silent is worse. When I finally found my voice and said "enough," I wasn't only fighting for myself. I was fighting for a team that depended on me and for the culture I wanted to create for my team. This was about me rejecting the old narratives that told me to stay quiet. Courage in leadership means standing up for what's right, even when it's uncomfortable. It's the only way real change happens

Success Is About the Collective, Not the Individual

Despite the hostility I faced in my defining moment, my team's success became my anchor and my joy. By focusing on their growth and well-being, I found purpose and strength. This reinforced the idea that leadership is not about personal accolades, but about creating environments where others can shine. Heart-centered leadership recognizes that the greatest measure of success is the collective impact of empowered, inspired people working toward a shared vision.

Leadership is measured by how you uplift those around you.

Staying Grounded Is Key to Sustainability

Yes, leadership is about uplifting others, but if you want to stay the course, it is necessary to stay grounded. In the whirlwind of keeping all the plates spinning, the ability to remain connected to your core values becomes your source of stability. For me, staying grounded has meant

- staying connected with my *why*
- practicing self-reflection to continuously grow
- aligning my values and my actions
- always returning to the belief that leadership is about people

At times, staying grounded was essential for survival and will be essential for future me to avoid returning to old patterns. When my dad passed away, I found myself navigating grief on a personal level while balancing my career responsibilities. In those moments, it was easy to feel untethered, as though the weight of everything would pull me under, but my core values kept me anchored.

The emphasis on staying grounded stands in stark contrast to command-and-control leadership, which by its very nature is centered around ego and positional power. The inflexibility in these leaders disconnects them from their teams and from their personal values. Replacing connection with control makes it difficult to stay grounded and decisions are driven by fear or ego rather than purpose and people. Heart-centered leadership naturally supports being grounded through self-awareness and intentionality in actions. It becomes contagious, sets the tone for the team, and encourages others to remain balanced and focused, even in challenging circumstances.

One particular frustrating experience that happened early in my consulting career tested my ability to stay grounded in the face of controlling leadership. My boss hired someone for my team who initially seemed competent, but eventually began to create friction within the group and with clients. When I decided his contract wouldn't be renewed, my boss dismissed my opinion and framed the issue as a failure in my leadership. His inability to step back and objectively assess the situation highlighted his preoccupation with authority over collaboration. He ignored the opinions of the paying clients and other team members, choosing instead to save face.

If he had taken the time to ground himself in the facts and trust my expertise, he would have recognized that no one was at fault; it was simply a situation where the hire didn't work out. Staying grounded also means recognizing when to step back and realign. Maintaining equilibrium between self-awareness and staying present is essential. Below are some practices that have proven effective for me.

- **Set Boundaries**. Early in my career, I felt the pressure to be available at all hours. Over time, I realized that setting clear boundaries was essential for my well-being. Protecting time for myself and my daughter allowed me to recharge and show up effectively at work.

- **Practice Self-Compassion**. Leadership comes with inevitable mistakes. Instead of dwelling on what I could have done better, I focused on learning from those moments and extending the same grace to myself that I offered to others. While I haven't mastered this completely, as a recovering perfectionist, I'm getting there.

- **Create a Support System**. I still rely on a network of trusted friends, mentors, and colleagues who provide advice, encouragement, and practical support when I need it most. In the past, knowing I wasn't alone made all the difference during challenging times.

- **Self-Care**. Meditation has become a daily practice for me, though it's usually the first thing I abandon when overwhelmed. (Yes, a very counterintuitive habit I'm working on.) Having consulted my psychotherapist when the toxicity became unbearable, she introduced me to heart-centered breathing and coherence techniques, which were transformative. Even during the most tense meetings in a toxic environment, I could use this coherence technique to remain calm and composed. Coherence was a gamechanger for me.

The Imposter Syndrome Cure

Addressing my imposter syndrome was key to changing my mindset. As a leader, addressing your imposter syndrome is a personal triumph, and it's a responsibility. Self-doubt can subtly influence leadership decisions, from withholding praise to hesitating when delegating meaningful tasks. When leaders confront their insecurities, they are better equipped to create environments that support their teams. By modeling confidence and vulnerability, leaders set the tone. How did I do this? Here are some tips on how I help my teams to address their self-doubt.

- **Normalize Conversations About Imposter Syndrome.** Regular check-ins during one-on-one meetings can help people discuss their progress and any self-doubts without making it a formal conversation or an overwhelming topic. Reassuring people that self-doubt is common reduces its power.

- **Recognize and Acknowledge Contributions.** Public and private recognition of people's efforts helps them counteract imposter syndrome's negative self-talk. Heart-centered leaders prioritize making their team members feel seen and appreciated.

- **Provide Constructive, Growth-Focused Feedback.** Praise is important, but so is supportive feedback framed as a development opportunity. A routine of constructive feedback helps individuals build confidence and encourages continuous learning.

- **Be Open About Your Own Struggles.** I have shared my own battles with self-doubt, and it reassures people that even successful leaders have moments of questioning themselves. Transparency creates trust and an environment that reassures people they are not alone.

In contrast, command-and-control leaders frequently exacerbate imposter syndrome by creating a culture of fear and insecurity. These leaders, who rely on rigid hierarchies and micromanagement, send an unconscious message that team members are not to be trusted to make decisions or take ownership of their work, perpetuating imposter syndrome. By sharing my efforts to overcome imposter syndrome, and by empowering and supporting my team, I was able to turn my own struggles into a foundation for collective strength.

Leading with Heart Beyond the Workplace

Transforming into leading from the heart isn't only about the workplace; it's about how we show up in every part of our lives. It's woven into our interactions with family, friends, communities, and even strangers. Leadership comes in many forms: organizing events, stepping up in a crisis, mentoring others, advocating for causes, or simply offering a helping hand to a neighbor. For me, these moments feel like second nature, but I also know that my understanding of leadership was shaped as much by negative experiences as it was by positive ones.

Let me start with an inspiring example. My neighbor, well into her retirement years, has never stopped leading in her own quiet, impactful way. Since I've known her, she's volunteered with the University of the Third Age, managing office administration and timetabling. She's served as secretary on several golfing committees while still playing a mean game herself. For years, she was the president of our body corporate, stepping up from the very first meeting and only recently stepping down after helping transform the committee and the complex into a well-run, thriving community. Beyond her formal leadership roles, I've watched her gently mentor and encourage many aspiring women in our neighborhood. She always seems to know when to ask a tough question to challenge my thinking and when to steer a conversation in a completely different direction. She was my go-to ear while I was battling my demons and going through defining moments, and I will always hold a dear place in my heart for her unwavering support. As if that isn't enough—she feeds my cat! When I let my neighbor read this, her response was authentic and in character: "I suppose I am a teacher at heart and naturally fall into a quasi-mentoring mode."

Now, contrast that with my childhood. My dad's need for control dictated how he interacted with everyone. There was no room for collaboration or shared success—only dominance. Some people appreciated his take-charge attitude because it meant they didn't have to take responsibility themselves, but others—including me—were humiliated by his authoritarian approach. I can still picture the way his leg would twitch when his aggression built, a tell-tale sign of the emotional storm about to erupt. His behavior embarrassed my mum, and I became an expert at making excuses for him, even when his actions left people crushed. He saw himself as a leader in his community, but in reality, his leadership was built on ego, control, and the constant need to be the center of attention.

When I became a single parent, I made a conscious decision never to humiliate my daughter the way I had been humiliated as a child. That decision shaped how I raised her but also how I approached leadership in my career. Difficult conversations were always handled in private and with respect. I never wanted anyone to feel small, powerless, or ashamed under my leadership.

These experiences, both positive and negative, demonstrate what natural leadership looks like. Leadership in the community is definitely not about titles or authority; it's about creating environments of success. Leadership happens in the smallest of moments, comforting a colleague, encouraging someone to think differently or challenging outdated norms that hold people back. Some of the most persuasive leaders don't have formal titles at all. Take Greta Thunberg, for example. She didn't wait for permission to lead; she stepped forward, spoke her truth, and inspired millions.

At its core, heart-centered leadership is about making a positive difference—one interaction at a time. Whether at home, in the community, or at work, the impact of this kind of leadership extends far beyond the immediate moment.

Leading from the heart creates ripples of lasting impact.

It All Started with Motherhood

For single parents, work-life balance is no luxury; it's survival. It's a constant, never-ending negotiation of time, energy, and priorities. Let's not sugarcoat it—it's exhausting, demanding, and, at times, overwhelming. It is also deeply rewarding. For me, balance was not about achieving perfection. I dreamed instead about making deliberate choices that aligned with my values and responsibilities. When I look back on those years, I see the exhaustion but also the growth. It was a time that honed my leadership style and revealed my superpower: resilience. Late nights were constant. Those evenings bled into early mornings, helping with school projects or navigating the latest teenage crisis. My career choices were deliberate, guided by the need to be present for my daughter. While imperfect, this time brought unexpected rewards. Necessity made me productive. Challenges sparked creativity. It was a fulfilling time of being both a fully present parent and a dedicated professional. Those moments of sitting up in bed together watching a movie or driving between sports events (endless sports events!) grounded me and reminded me why I was working so hard.

Workplaces of the time weren't designed for this kind of balance. The culture didn't support family life, especially for single working mums. In roles where I couldn't bring work home due to its sensitive nature, I regularly had to leave my daughter alone, simply because I had exhausted my sick leave. I saw organizations that rewarded the *illusion* of dedication—where staying late for the sake of appearances was praised higher than actual productivity. I remember one particular workplace where long coffee breaks and extended lunches went unnoticed, yet my efficiency, eating lunch at my desk so I could leave on time, was met with raised eyebrows and silent judgment. My commitment was questioned, despite my results speaking for themselves.

The financial sacrifices from those years still linger. Prioritizing my daughter over climbing the corporate ladder meant turning down higher-paying jobs that would have required me to be away from her more. Decades later, I still feel the weight of those decisions: a mortgage larger than it should be at this stage of my life, and career opportunities that pass me by because I didn't have the finances to pursue an MBA. When I look at my daughter who is now a genuine, kind, and capable leader in her own right, every difficult decision is validated, and I wouldn't change anything. Those years shaped my strength, but motherhood is where my leadership philosophy incubated.

Being a mum taught me that authority is less impressive than empathy. It taught me an understanding of people as whole, complex individuals, each navigating their own challenges. Despite the growing understanding of the importance of empathy in leadership, outdated models persist, prioritizing direction and competition over connection and teamwork. Watching my daughter navigate her own leadership journey in a world that remains resistant to change has only deepened my resolve to keep pushing for something better. Like me, she battles rigid systems and outdated expectations. Seeing her fight those battles reinforces my belief that leadership must continue to evolve, that we must move toward valuing people and purpose over power and control.

As I continue to advocate for change in leadership, I've instilled in her the belief that she has the power to create change too. Her successes and struggles reflect a journey that spans two generations, each working toward the same goal—a world where leadership is rooted in humanity, *not hierarchy*.

I realize that, in my role as a mum, passing lessons to my daughter is one crucial responsibility, but it's equally as important to me to pass them on to everyone I have the privilege to lead.

Figure 12: In Sydney for Lydia's twenty-first birthday

"The moment anyone tries to demean you in any way, you have to know how great you are. Nobody would bother to beat you down if you were not a threat."

—Cicely Tyson, actress known for her portrayal of complex and strong-willed African American women

MY INNER TRANSFORMATION

"There's no wrong place to start on the journey of expansion. Simply let your heart guide you to the starting point and begin."

—Anne Ligthart, psychotherapist

Figure 13: Me and my brother on a family holiday, taken in 1975

Jon's Story: A Journey to Leadership Coaching

Jon never set out to work in leadership development. In fact, his journey began with a geography degree, simply because that was his interest. His early career took him through a brief stint in stockbroking, where he had a realization: finance wasn't really about numbers—it was about people. That realization sparked something in him, leading him to take a role in an organization within the National Australia Bank group.

For years, Jon found himself in roles that didn't quite fit. The bank offered him opportunities, but each time, he experienced a growing disconnect between the job demands and what honestly mattered to him. That misalignment created an internal struggle, leading to anxiety, guilt, and shame. He felt he was in the wrong place, yet he continued pushing forward because he didn't think he had other choices. The organization was supportive in many ways, providing him with opportunities and investing in his growth. Twenty-two years into his career, Jon was appointed into a senior role, which involved an unexpectedly high level of project management responsibility, which was well outside his skill set. The anxiety intensified, and the sense of ineffectiveness weighed heavily on him. He reached a point where something had to change.

Finally, Jon made the decision to speak up. He went to his general manager and admitted he was in the wrong role. He needed to step aside and allow someone else to take on the project management work. To Jon's relief, his honesty was met with understanding. His manager didn't push him away; instead, he supported Jon by arranging a coach, and alongside one of Jon's mentors, they explored the fundamental questions: "Who am I? What are my strengths? What excites me? What opportunities exist that align with those strengths?" Jon's mentor took a different approach—rather than focusing on weaknesses, which had been Jon's career development focus to that date, they concentrated on what Jon naturally excelled at. From that, Jon began to shape a new path. He quite literally sketched out a plan on paper, drawing four boxes with arrows connecting them. That simple visual representation became the blueprint for his future: coaching, mentoring, facilitation, and leadership development.

Jon had no intention of leaving the organization, and through networking and conversations, he was steered toward an internal consulting role in another part of the company. That move changed everything. For the first time in his career, he felt aligned with his work. He was no longer struggling to fit into a role that didn't suit him; instead, he was thriving. For seven years, he immersed himself in leadership development, coaching and team development. Then, ready for the next chapter, he took the leap and started his own business. Nearly nine years later, he is still doing what he loves. His work doesn't feel like a job—it's a vocation. He regularly reflects on how fortunate he is, getting to do this work.

Adapting to Leadership Development

Jon attributes much of his development to the bank's investment in him. They funded his training at the Institute of Executive Coaching and Leadership, and later, they sent him to the Harvard Kennedy School for a program called the Art and Practice of Leadership Development. It was there he was introduced to adaptive leadership, a framework developed by Ron Heifetz and Marty Linsky at Harvard University. "Adaptive leadership," he explains, "is about mobilizing people to tackle their toughest challenges and thrive. It shifts the focus from management to leadership as an activity—something anyone, at any level, can engage in. Leadership isn't about titles or hierarchy; it's about facilitating change."

Jon sees adaptive leadership as an overarching philosophy that ties together various leadership theories. The Kansas Leadership Center encapsulates this idea by simplifying it to "just leadership"—a set of principles that remain constant regardless of context. In his view, authority, management, and leadership each serve distinct purposes. Authority is granted based on position, expertise, or experience. Management is about maintaining order and the efficient use of resources. Leadership, quite distinctly, is about driving change.

"The essence of leadership is understanding that change involves loss, and people don't fear change itself—they fear what they might lose in the process. A leader's role, then, is to help people navigate loss, making it clear that the transition is worthwhile." Whether it's an organization adapting to artificial intelligence, restructuring teams, or shifting cultural norms, the principles of leadership remain the same: mobilize people, listen, connect, and empower others to take responsibility for progress. "The solution to complex adaptive challenges doesn't come from the person at the top, it's from everybody. The leadership job is to get everyone on board. Heart-centered leadership would be the part that engages people in a way that they are enthusiastic, energized and willing to put in discretionary effort."

When discussing command-and-control leadership, Jon acknowledges that there are moments when it is necessary: "in emergencies, disasters, and high-stakes crises where immediate decisions must be made. However, in day-to-day organizational life, that style is counterproductive." True authority in these situations isn't about giving orders; it's about earning trust. People follow authorities in crises, not simply because they hold a title, but when they trust that authority to provide direction, protection, and order.

Leadership, Jon believes, can be developed. While some people may have a natural inclination for it, leadership skills can be taught and refined. His approach is experiential, allowing people to develop their leadership capabilities through action rather than theory. He also recognizes the risks that come with leadership. "Speaking up, challenging the status quo, and pushing for change can make people uncomfortable." Leaders become targets. Greta Thunberg, for example, embodies what happens when someone steps up to lead—she mobilizes people around a cause, but in doing so, she also faces intense scrutiny and criticism.

"Women, in particular, face unique challenges in leadership," Jon points out that societal norms expect women to be agreeable and deferential, qualities that do not always align with the activities of leadership. When people assert themselves, they are frequently criticized for their style rather than their substance, and unfairly, this is disproportionately true for women. "Key to the exercise of leadership," he says, "is choice—knowing when to stand up or stand firm, and when to adapt, because ultimately, it's more important to be able to stay on the field, than to be taken off it."

Jon's journey is a testament to the power of self-awareness, adaptability, and purpose-driven leadership. He found his way, not by conforming to traditional career expectations, but by understanding his strengths and aligning his work with his passion. Now, through coaching and leadership development, he helps others do the same.

> "Failure is an important part of your growth and developing resilience. Don't be afraid to fail."
>
> —Michelle Obama, attorney, mother, former US first lady

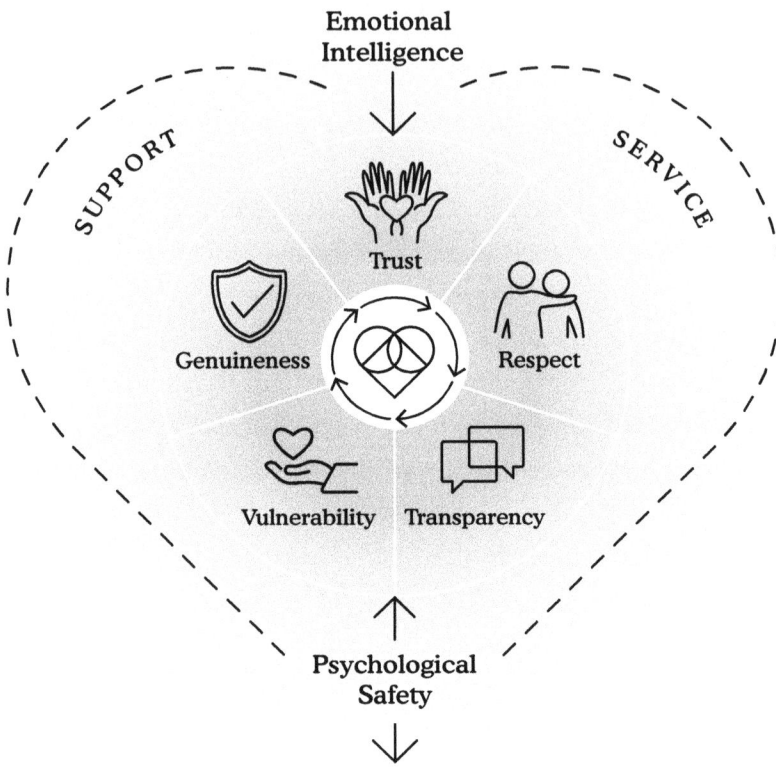

Figure 14: Revisiting the Heart-Centered Leadership Model

6

A Practical Guide to Leading with Heart

How to Lead with Heart

Here we are, at the chapter where you get to take over. Leadership has long been tied back to the Industrial Revolution–era concepts of authority, control, and strategy. For decades, we've been told that strong leaders need to be tough, that they need to be in control, make the hard calls, and push people toward results. I hope now that you are this far into my story, you have come to the realization that heart-centered leadership isn't about having all the answers or being the loudest voice in the room; it's about creating an environment where people can bring their best selves to work. It's about making leadership less about ego and more about impact. It isn't reserved for a select few. You don't have to be a certain personality type, have a specific title, or be born with some innate ability. Heart-centered leadership can be a choice—a conscious decision to lead with purpose and humanity. It's about showing up as your real, imperfect, human self and creating space for others to do the same.

However, I'll be honest, this isn't for everyone. Some people thrive in environments where hierarchy and control rule the day. I couldn't be a domineering, egotistical leader even if I tried. It's not who I am. I have my doubts that leaders who rely on fear and manipulation can truly lead from the heart. Can emotional intelligence be learned? Maybe. If it's completely absent, I'm not sure you can fake it forever. I've met my fair share of corporate megalomaniac who can put on a convincing act of empathy, but their actions always give them away in the end. That said, most leaders aren't in that extreme category. Many genuinely want to lead in a way that feels meaningful, but they don't always know how. That's what this chapter is for.

This is a practical guide, a real-world, actionable way to become a heart-centered leader. You choose your journey: whether you're stepping into leadership for the first time or looking to shift the way you manage people, this chapter will walk you through some actionable steps to make heart-centered leadership real in your everyday life.

If you're ready to lead differently, let's get started.

Firstly, a reminder of the essential elements that are key to my heart-centered leadership model: trust, respect, vulnerability, transparency, and genuineness, built on the pillars of service and support, and thriving in an environment of psychological safety and emotional intelligence.

- **Trust** is built through acting consistently, following through on commitments, and demonstrating integrity, enabling people to feel safe to do their best work.
- **Genuineness** is being true to yourself and leading with sincerity to build deeper connections and stronger teams.
- **Respect** means valuing each team member's contributions, ideas, and individuality to create an empowered and inclusive workplace.
- **Transparency** includes sharing openly and respectfully to build credibility, honest dialogue, and ensuring people have all the information they need to be successful.
- **Vulnerability** is embodied by admitting mistakes and acknowledging that not all the answers are available to create a space for collaboration and problem-solving.
- **Support** is the structure that enables people to grow, experiment, and reach their potential.
- **Service** includes the mindset that leadership is about uplifting, guiding, and empowering others.
- **Psychological Safety** creates an environment that is safe for people to ask questions, share concerns, admit mistakes, and experiment without fear of humiliation or punishment.
- **Emotional Intelligence** is recognizing and understanding our own emotions while effectively responding to the emotions of others.

Now that we've reestablished the foundation of heart-centered leadership, it's time to shift gears—from understanding the *what* to applying the *how*. Theory is one thing, but leadership is built through action. This chapter doesn't give you a rigid formula. There's no exact timeline, no perfect sequence to follow. Heart-centered leadership isn't about ticking boxes; it's about intentional action, small adjustments, and a commitment to continuous learning.

The actions that follow are intended as starting points to guide you, not box you in. You don't need to follow them in the precise order or within a set timeframe. That said, it makes sense to begin with *self*. Once you feel you've made some progress there—not perfection or mastery—the natural progression is to focus on leading others, and then on shaping culture.

But again, this is not a linear journey. Leadership development is deeply personal. What works for one person may unfold completely differently for another. This work is cyclical, adaptable, and entirely yours to shape. What you'll need to get started:

- a diary or planner, something to record your thoughts, observations, and progress
- a willingness to experiment, fail, and reflect because this process isn't about getting it right the first time
- an appetite to unlearn by letting go of practices, beliefs, and ideas that no longer serve you
- courage because this journey is going to be uncomfortable at times

Leading with heart in environments that have long rewarded power and control can feel vulnerable—even exposing. You may feel resistance, both from yourself and from those around you. That's OK. Lean into that discomfort. Growth is never comfortable, but it is always worth it.

Figure 15: Heart-Centered Leadership Guided Learning

A small note: We discussed creating psychological safety as a leader at length in chapter 3, and you will see those tips integrated into these actions. We also discussed the dangers of starting something then abandoning it, so ask yourself, "Am I ready?"

Another small note: At the time of writing this, *The Heart-Centered Leader Workbook* is in development.

Making a Start: Turning Intentions to Actions

I recommend setting monthly goals and actions—small, tangible steps that help you bring heart-centered leadership to life. At the end of each week, take a moment to reflect on what worked and what didn't. If you're unsure where to start your self-reflections, consider:

- Where did I lead with heart this week?
- What was one moment my actions truly aligned with my values?

- Where did I hesitate or fall into old habits?
- How did others respond to me differently?
- What is one small shift I can make next week?

Don't reflect on your actions only. Pay attention to how others respond to you. Are your team members open, engaged, or willing to share ideas? Are your peers showing trust or seeking your input differently? Has your own leader's attitude toward you changed? These subtle shifts can reveal the impact of your transformation more than anything else.

It's also critical to note your own reactions. How does it feel when people respond to you differently? Do you feel confident? More at ease? Are you struggling with the discomfort of being seen in a new way? Recognizing these emotional shifts is crucial because leadership is about how you influence others, how you allow yourself to be influenced and grow by the change you create.

The key here is not to judge yourself. Growth isn't linear. Some months you'll feel like you've made incredible progress, and others, you'll feel like you've taken two steps back. That's normal. Reset at the beginning of the next month, adjust as needed, and keep going. Don't forget to acknowledge your wins, even the small ones. Change takes effort, and recognizing your progress along the way is as important as setting the goals themselves. This is your journey, and how you go about it is up to you. If you're ready to walk this talk, know this: things are about to change. If you stick with it, those changes won't only transform your leadership.

They'll transform you.

Now, let's get started on those actions.

Lead Self

Cultivate Self-Awareness and Emotional Intelligence

Heart-centered leadership requires you to understand yourself—your triggers, strengths, and areas for growth. Leaders who lack self-awareness can unintentionally create environments of fear or disengagement. It is important to be clear who you are and to understand your own values, beliefs, and emotions. This goes hand in hand with emotional intelligence, a quality that enables you to manage your emotions, read the room, and respond rather than react.

What This Looks Like in Practice

→ *Action:* Reflect on your current leadership style—are you directive, collaborative, or somewhere in between? How do your natural tendencies show up under pressure, during conflict, and through ambiguity? Do you default to control? Then, take a step back. How does your leadership impact those around you?

→ *Action:* Identify your core values and ensure your actions align with them. JamesClear.com has a wonderful starting-point list of core values for people to review. Pick your top five. I recently redid mine after four years. I was curious if they had changed through recent experiences; some stayed the same, but some certainly changed.

→ *Action:* Seek feedback from your team and colleagues through casual conversation, but don't make it too formal. Genuinely listen to what they say. This can be tough, so avoid becoming defensive and avoid beating yourself up. I recommend doing breathing exercises if you feel a little anxious before you enter into these conversations.

Show Vulnerability and Let Go of Control

Letting go is hard! You've worked hard to build your expertise, and it can feel risky to trust someone with the results. Holding on too tightly limits your team, and it limits you. Micromanagement destroys trust, undermines autonomy, and stifles creativity. For your team to operate with independence and continue growing, you must be willing to loosen your grip. This is crucial in times of ambiguity or change. It's a common leadership trap to think you need to have all the answers or tightly control the direction, but solving complex problems demands collaboration. The best path forward emerges from inviting more minds into the process, not fewer.

To lead in this way, you need to embrace vulnerability. By sharing your own challenges and uncertainties, you show your team that imperfection is all part of growth. When leaders demonstrate vulnerability, they invite respect. This will probably feel uncomfortable, especially if you're used to being hands-on, but remember, we are embracing experimentation and learning through experience. The more you model that mindset, the more your team will feel safe to step up, speak out, and shape the future *with* you.

How to Let Go

→ *Action:* Take some time to self-reflect on one thing that you are currently holding onto too tightly.

→ *Action:* Delegate with trust, not suspicion—give people real ownership, don't give them tasks to perform; let them own it, but remember to support them with clarity, guidance, and resources.

→ *Action:* Encourage innovation—let people experiment without the fear of harsh consequences. If it doesn't work out, use it as a learning experience and unpack what happened and what was learned.

→ *Action:* Focus on coaching rather than dictating—ask guiding questions instead of giving direct orders. Instead of pretending you have the answers, try saying, "I don't have the perfect solution, but let's figure it out together."

→ *Action:* Celebrate and elevate people's strengths—help them see their potential and build confidence in their capabilities.

Lead Others

Build Connections Through Being Present

Leaders, by the very nature of the job, have to manage tasks; great leaders also build relationships. When you meet with people, be present both physically and mentally, be genuinely attentive and emotionally available. When people feel valued and respected, they are naturally more engaged and committed; when you give your full attention to them, they feel safe to express themselves. Showing respect reinforces trust. Treating people with genuine dignity is a moral imperative, but also a driver of belonging. Teams flourish when individuals feel valued and respected for who they are, not only for what they produce. However, respect must be authentic. "Faking it till you make it" will backfire. People can sense a lack of genuineness, and without it, respect cannot grow.

Ways to Strengthen Connection

→ *Action:* Prioritize active listening—give your undivided, clear attention to hear what is being said without interrupting or formulating responses in your head. It means putting your phone away so you can't be distracted and maintaining eye contact so the other person sees your respect.

→ *Action:* Check in regularly with your team—yes, about their work but more importantly, include conversations about their well-being and aspirations. These conversations don't need to be deeply personal or invasive; presence doesn't mean prying. Show them how much their work life and career matter to you, show genuine interest in their growth.

→ *Action:* Show up with genuineness—be engaged in conversations, meetings, and decisions. Whether in person or online, people can sense when you're distracted. Avoid multitasking and respectfully excuse yourself if you have to take an important call. This is especially important—if not more so—for remote or hybrid teams.

→ *Action:* Recognize contributions meaningfully. Generic praise can be tokenistic; rather, highlight specific efforts and impact. Make a reward plan, for example, "The chocolate bar of the week goes to..." In one project, my team gave posters to workshop participants; the posters became a sought-after item, and participation increased. The posters simply said a popular five-word motivational phrase.

Support with Empathy and Service

I have always considered removing roadblocks as my number-one job as a leader. This is very necessary so the bigger job can get done and the team is set up for success; this is my service to them. Heart-centered leaders understand that part of their role is service, as well as understanding the impact that service has on creating loyalty and respect. When teams are set up to organize themselves and have a mindset for continuous improvements, I can stay on the balcony and focus on driving strategy and steering the ship. Empathy and service are intertwined; together they provide the necessary condition to understand and connect with the needs and the feelings of people.

How to Lead with Service

→ *Action:* Show that you care in those rarely missed one-on-ones by asking, "How can I help you succeed?" instead of "What can you do for me?" Reframing this question shifts the conversation from transactional and shows that you're invested in their growth, not only their output.

→ *Action:* Remove obstacles that prevent your team from doing their best work. How can you determine what the roadblocks are? Something else to ask in those rarely missed one-on-one sessions.

→ *Action:* Publicly advocate for your people by supporting their growth, providing development opportunities, and calling out their contributions to the wider organization. This can be really uncomfortable for a lot of people when trying to break from a top-down environment. It is certainly easier to agree with people around you and not rock the boat (especially if you are walking on those eggshells), but sometimes you have to hold the mirror up to power and fight for your team. This is another time to avoid defensiveness.

→ *Action:* Model integrity and accountability. Do what you say, say what you do, and hold yourself to the same standards you expect from everyone else. When you make a commitment of any size, honor it, and if something changes, communicate transparently. This demonstrates to your people what accountability looks like in practice.

Lead Culture

Create Psychological Safety through Transparency and Trust

A team without trust operates in survival mode—people second-guess decisions, hesitate to speak up, and fear the consequences of making mistakes. They "tread lightly." In a psychological safe team, people feel confident to experiment, share ideas, and challenge assumptions without fear of retribution. I once worked in an environment where speaking up in meetings seemed like a high-risk move because people had seen colleagues shut down before, so most kept their ideas to themselves. To shift this in my meetings, I made a conscious effort to show that honesty was more than accepted—it was valued. I started by acknowledging every contribution with phrases like "Thank you for sharing that," or "That's a refreshing perspective." I also encouraged diverse thinking by openly appreciating ideas that challenged the norm: "It's great to hear something out of left field—it gets us thinking in new ways."

It was equally important to address resistance in a way that kept the conversation open. When a naysayer pushed back, I reinforced that all opinions were welcome while setting the tone for respectful debate: "I appreciate a different perspective, but let's not slip into being personal." Over time, these small shifts transformed my team meetings, people began speaking up and robust discussions became the norm. If your meetings feel one-sided or silent, consider how people in the room react when others share their ideas. A simple change in language and intentional encouragement can make all the difference in creating a space where everyone feels safe to contribute.

Actions Toward Building Psychological Safety

→ *Action:* Normalize open and constructive dialogue. Invite different perspectives and ideas. Be present and practice active listening. In chapter 3, we talked about requesting "Tell me more about what is on your mind," rather than jumping in with a solution.

→ *Action:* Model vulnerability by admitting when you're wrong, seeking feedback (even when it is uncomfortable). Demonstrate that learning is valued. Vulnerability is an essential builder of trust. When leaders acknowledge their mistakes or uncertainties, it gives others permission to do the same.

→ *Action:* Demonstrate consistency. People need to know they can count on you to act with integrity. Psychological safety flourishes when there are no surprises in how a leader shows up. If your values shift based on who's in the room or what's convenient, trust in your leadership will erode. When people see that your words align with your behavior, they will feel safe to contribute, challenge, and grow.

→ *Action:* Remove fear of failure. Shift your team's mindset from "Who is to blame?" to "What can we learn?" Use the overworked phrase "Let's draw a line in the sand!" to move conversations forward respectfully. There is a reason that phrase is overused.

One Bite at a Time

As you start to journal and plan, keep in mind that this journey isn't about achieving perfection—it's about showing up, leading with heart, and making a difference one conversation, one decision, and one moment at a time. It's about embracing lifelong learning. This isn't a quick fix or a leadership trend. It's an ongoing commitment to being the kind of leader who goes beyond managing people to being one who materially, quantifiably impacts them. It's about leading in a way that makes people feel seen, valued, and inspired to show up at work as their best selves.

Let's acknowledge something important: this shift in leadership style can be confronting, especially if you have spent years in systems that rewarded control and positional power. It's natural to feel fear: fear of losing influence, of being vulnerable, or of not being taken seriously. These fears are valid, as I regularly say to myself, "They can visit my brain, but they are not allowed to make a home there."

The antidote to fear is having faith in your ability to grow, adapt, and lead from your heart. You won't have all the answers, and you don't need to. You don't need to become a perfect leader overnight or ever—that's impossible. What matters is your willingness to begin. You are going to fail but have faith in yourself. Stay connected to your purpose, surround yourself with people who lift you up, and reflect on your progress regularly. You're more capable than you think.

Heart-centered leadership has a wide-ranging impact; it affects workplaces and influences culture; it changes people. It builds trust where there was fear. It creates connection where there was isolation. It turns leadership from a position of power into a force for growth, purpose, and transformation. As you take these steps, reflect often, adjust when needed, and give yourself the grace to learn along the way. It won't always be easy, but it will always be worth it.

Ask yourself:
- How do I want people to feel under my leadership?
- What kind of leader do I aspire to be?
- Am I ready to lead with my whole heart?

Now, it's time to act. Lead with courage. Lead with integrity. Lead with heart.

Because when you do, you're not merely leading—you're creating a legacy.

> ## "She stood in the storm, and when the wind did not blow her away, she adjusted her sails."
>
> —Elizabeth Edwards, author and health care activist

Figure 16: Me at 9 months old with my mum

7

Where is Leadership Headed?

Looking Back: A Journey Through Leadership and Growth

As I write this final chapter, I find myself reflecting on the journey that brought us here—the stories, the lessons, the opportunities, and the empowerment that shaped not only this book but my entire life and leadership philosophy.

When I first set out to write this book, I wasn't interested in producing another leadership book filled with theories, corporate jargon, or one-size-fits-all advice. No, this book has been much more personal. It has been about truth, about peeling back the layers of what leadership looks like for me, not what I read in textbooks. It has been about the real, raw, and sometimes painful lessons that life has thrown my way. Lessons that tested me, broke me, and ultimately, rebuilt me into the leader and the person I am today.

We began this journey by diving into the world of command-and-control leadership, a style I came to recognize early in my life, first at home, then in the workplace. I grew up in an environment where authority was absolute, where questioning was seen as defiance, and where control was mistaken for strength. As I stepped into the business world, I quickly realized: control does not inspire; it suffocates. I saw firsthand how toxic workplaces drained talent, crushed confidence, and forced people to shrink themselves to fit into rigid boxes of expectation.

I also saw something else: the power of a different kind of leadership. A style that wasn't rooted in fear but in trust. A leadership style that didn't demand compliance but encouraged contribution. A leadership style that put people at the center, rather than power. This was the moment I began my transition from a world of command-and-control to something more potent—leading from the heart.

Throughout this book, we've explored the impact of leadership in all its forms—the good, the bad, and the transformational. We've seen how leaders build people up or tear them down, how cultures either nurture talent or push it away, and how organizations that fail to evolve lose their grip in a rapidly changing world. Leadership is changing, whether organizations are ready for it or not. We've unpacked some research, we've told the stories, and we've met people who lived through the highs and lows of life and leadership. People who, like me, have had to unlearn damaging lessons from the past and build their own approach to leadership from the ground up.

The future belongs to leaders who listen, not dictate, who empower, not control. To leaders who recognize that their success is measured not by how much power they wield, but by how many people they lift along the way.

But it's not changing quickly enough. A young woman I know approached me recently; she knew I was writing this book. She wanted to share her story of being the only female leader on an otherwise all-male leadership team. Under the weight of discrimination, exclusion, and constant undermining by her manager and peers—she was even asked to do the printing—she began to doubt herself. Her contributions were dismissed, and she became the target of blame. The pressure became unbearable—so much so that she found herself rewriting every email, second-guessing every word, and falling silent in meetings to avoid ridicule. Eventually, the stress took its toll, and she was no longer able to work.

Help came in the guise of a heart-centered leader from another part of the organization who heard what was happening—not through formal channels but through the grapevine. She chose not to believe the narrative she'd been fed, having worked with this young woman before. Instead, she reached out with empathy and offered her an immediate transfer. More than that, she offered her a safe space to heal, to be seen, and to rebuild her confidence.

That outreached hand meant so much. What a great example of the difference a heart-centered leader can make.

As we move forward in this ever-changing world into the future of leadership, I ask you to reflect on your own journey

- What kind of leader do you want to be?
- How do you want people to feel under your leadership?
- What kind of legacy do you want to leave?

Leadership is absolutely about what you do, but what we have learned throughout this book is that it's also about how you make people feel. If there's one thing I hope you take away from this book, it's this: **Leadership isn't about being in charge; it's about taking care of those in your charge.**

Where Do We Go from Here?

The future of leadership is being rewritten before our eyes. We're at a turning point. So what does the future look like? The answer lies in approaches that prioritize people, adaptability, and long-term impact. Emotional intelligence (EQ) has long been recognized as essential for effective leadership, but its relevance will be profound in the future of work. As businesses and organizations navigate increasing complexity, shifting workforce expectations, and the rapid pace of change, leaders must develop a deeper awareness of themselves and those around them.

At its core, emotional intelligence is the ability to recognize, understand, and regulate emotions—both in ourselves and in others. In leadership, EQ goes beyond self-awareness—it's about creating environments where people feel psychologically safe, valued, and motivated to do their best work, making them better equipped to handle conflict, drive engagement, and sustain long-term success.

Leadership is no longer about hitting performance targets above all else; it's progressed into being about creating an environment where people can bring their best selves to work *and* hit the targets. The future of leadership depends on leaders who can balance rational decision-making with emotional insight. Leaders need to understand that productivity is not merely about efficiency but about engagement. When people feel emotionally connected to their work, their colleagues, and their leaders, they perform better, stay longer, and contribute meaningfully.

Leading from the heart could be categorized as a "soft skill;" however, I see it as a core leadership capability that will define the future of work across all industries and cultures. Organizations that embrace this style of leadership will cultivate workplaces built to innovate, collaborate and succeed.

Why Does It Make Good Business Sense?

The workforce has changed. People are questioning everything—how they work, who they work for, and whether it's worth the emotional cost. They're craving leadership that feels human. That sees them. That listens. That respects their time, their energy, and their dignity. I've worked in organizations where this shift started to take root, and the difference is visible. People look out for each other. They get stuff done, not because they're afraid of the boss, but because they believe in the work and in each other.

So why heart-centered leadership?

This leadership style not only promotes a positive organizational culture, it delivers tangible results that directly impact success. Genuineness and trust are foundational for effective collaboration and open communication. When people feel seen, valued and heard, their connection to their work deepens. Heart-centered leaders understand individual needs and aspirations, which leads to higher job satisfaction and better engagement.

That engagement flows through the organization. Productivity increases. Staff stay longer. The revolving door slows down, and so do the hidden costs of replacing, retraining, and recovering from poor leadership. By creating a positive work environment, overall performance is enhanced, and organizations build strong foundations to experience sustainable success.

Leaders who lead with heart also set the tone for ethical behavior. As *Ellevate* eloquently states, this approach encourages employees to act with integrity and align with the organization's values. Over time, that shapes a socially responsible culture, enhancing the company's reputation and stakeholder trust.

Therefore, adopting a style of leading from the heart is a strategic decision that aligns with today's organizations, which are in constant change. Enhancing engagement, upholding ethical standards, and building for sustainable success, heart-centered leadership proves to be a transformative approach that benefits both individuals and the organization as a whole.

So yes, leading from the heart is good for morale, but it's also a good business strategy, especially in a world where disruption and change is constant, where people are your greatest asset. Heart-centered leadership is a roadmap for sustainable success.

Heart-Centered and Systems Leadership

Disruption and change don't simply pop up from time to time—they're part of the everyday landscape in business and life. For today's leaders (and definitely for tomorrow's), that means learning to navigate complexity and guide others through with clarity, connection, and purpose.

No leader operates in a vacuum. Everything is connected—people, teams, departments, organizations, industries, and broader social and economic systems. That's why we need leadership that understands these connections and knows how to work with them, not against them. That's where systems leadership comes in. At its heart, systems leadership is about seeing the bigger picture. It's rooted in systems thinking, which means looking beyond your silo and noticing how everything interacts. How decisions ripple outward, how challenges can be more complex than they appear, and how we can create lasting change by working with the system rather than trying to control it. Systems leaders ask, *What's really going on here?* They see relationships, patterns, interdependencies. And because of that, they anticipate problems instead of reacting to them.

Instead of micromanaging, they create the conditions for collaboration and trust. They build ecosystems, not empires. Sounds like a perfect overlap with heart-centered leadership. Both approaches lean on emotional intelligence—not authority—for influence. Both prioritize people, connection, and trust. And both understand that lasting change doesn't happen because someone at the top said so—it happens when you shift enough hearts and minds to move in a new direction together. What does this intersection look like in practice?

- **Zooming Out to See the System.** It's about noticing how things connect—how different parts of the organization impact each other—and working to bring people out of their silos. Generally that means digging into messy, adaptive problems that don't have simple fixes.

- **Collaboration Over Control.** It means getting curious, asking questions, and drawing in a wide range of voices. The more perspectives at the table, the stronger the solution, understanding that the best answers frequently come from the most unexpected places.

- **Sitting with the Unknown.** You don't need all the answers. In fact, being OK with not having them is part of the work. As is navigating gray areas and helping others stay grounded when things feel uncertain.

- **Leading Through Influence.** True transformation doesn't come from telling people what to do—it comes from connection: building trust, listening deeply, and engaging people in the change. It's about supporting people to move forward, not pushing them.

The old-school mindset says, *If you want to change a system, you have to control it.* But that's outdated. Today's best leaders know that if you want to change a system, you start by influencing the people within it. Support enough people to think differently, to act differently—and the whole system begins to shift.

This kind of influence comes from what my granddad demonstrated decades earlier: using your head and your heart. It's not about being soft. It's about being smart *and* human. It's about creating an environment where people feel safe, valued, and trusted—so they can bring their best ideas forward without fear and their whole selves to work.

Heart-centered leadership is about building strong teams, but it is more than that—it's about shaping entire organizations to operate with compassion, purpose, and sustainable success. The leaders who embrace this model know that trust and well-being are essentials for long-term business performance, higher staff retention, greater innovation, and better relationships all around. What do organizations look like when heart-centered leadership meets systems thinking?

- They have a culture of *really* listening—not performative nodding, but listening where people actually feel heard and understood.

- They're genuine. No corporate masks, no fake leadership personas—genuine people leading with purpose.

- They create psychological safety. People are free to speak up, experiment, own their mistakes, and learn out loud so the whole organization can grow.

- They celebrate success and failure—they act on lessons that come from things that went well and things that didn't go to plan. Growth is the goal.

This is the future—deeply human, strategically smart, and grounded in the belief that when people flourish, organizations do too.

The Cost of Silence: Ending the Criminalization of Speaking Up

Throughout this book, I have shared stories of people who faced bullying and narcissism in the workplace. Apart from having this in common, there is one other thread: the bullied were forced out of organizations, and the bullies were protected. The bullied people had to leave, heal, and pick their lives back up, typically with career and financial consequences. This is why there is an unspoken rule in many organizations: stay silent or suffer the consequences. Too often, people don't speak out against workplace bullying, toxic leadership, or unethical behavior because the system protects the perpetrator. The reality? As we have heard through these stories, the victim is punished while the bully remains untouched. What is the real incident rate and impact of bullying if it goes unreported?

Organizations must stop criminalizing those who speak up; nothing will change while this still happens. Cultures of silence not only perpetuate toxic workplaces but also push out the very people who have courage to demand better and instigate change. This isn't about ethics alone; it's about organizational success. Companies that welcome open dialogue, encourage constructive dissent, and protect those who challenge harmful behaviors improve the organizational culture, which in turn helps retain talent.

- **Leaders must set the tone.** If leadership punishes those who tell the truth, the message is clear: honesty is unwelcome. When leaders reward courage and transparency, they create a culture of trust and respect.
- **Psychological safety is key.** Employees need to know they can voice concerns without fear of retaliation. Otherwise, problems fester in the shadows, only surfacing when it's too late.
- **Accountability must be equal.** Protecting toxic leaders and executives at the expense of workplace culture is a short-term gain with long-term damage. Leadership must hold everyone to the same standard—regardless of rank.

Leadership shouldn't be about avoiding discomfort. Instead, lean into it and make the tough call. The future of leadership must embrace transparency, accountability, and a commitment to ending cultures of silence, of bullying, of victim blaming.

The Ripple Effect

Through this journey, I've learned that every hurdle I have encountered held the potential for strength and growth. The challenges I faced—both personal and professional—did not break me; they built me. I witnessed the ripple effect of my transformation as my teams thrived, my voice grew stronger, and I began to rewrite the narrative of what leadership could and should be. What started as an internal shift, extended outward, creating a positive feedback loop that empowered those around me, not only in the workplace.

My approach to heart-centered leadership is the embodiment of my life's experiences and my inner transformation. This transformation—from fear to empowerment, from struggle to strength, from isolation to connection—is how we create workplaces and futures where everyone has the chance to succeed. Its impact is not confined to individual leaders; it becomes contagious, spreading across teams, organizations and communities. Inner transformation doesn't simply benefit individuals, it creates a ripple effect that extends far beyond. As I've grown, I've seen how my journey influenced those around me. By leading with respect, vulnerability, and empathy, I create environments where others feel inspired to embrace their own journey of growth and lead with their hearts. I see team members begin to challenge assumptions, support one another, and innovate without fear of failure. All because they feel safe, valued, and empowered.

Going back to my mathematical roots: this ripple effect is akin to the butterfly effect of chaos theory, which tells us that small changes have big consequences. This is the essence of heart-centered leadership; it is about creating spaces where people are encouraged to contribute their best selves. When leaders commit to leading from the heart, they unleash a cycle of growth and inspiration that reshapes organizations. It starts with one person, but its impact is limitless. As I reflect, I am filled with a sense of hope.

I hope that by leading from the heart, we inspire others to do the same, sparking waves of positive change that carry far beyond what we see.

Gratitude

I owe a lot of gratitude to many people—so much so that I could never capture it all on one page. But I'll give it my best shot.

First, thank you to the brave, anonymous individuals who shared their journeys of bullying, narcissism, and leadership. I truly enjoyed speaking with every one of you, and I am grateful for your openness and contributions to this book.

A huge thank you to the generous souls who gave their time to review my book and offer invaluable feedback: Louise McGuiness, Valentina Mozetic, Sally Cunningham, Heidi van Rijswijk, Sophie Dodd, Katie Stanley, and Anastatia Contos. Your insight and support helped shape my thoughts and give me confidence, and I am so appreciative.

Thank you to Jon Eddy, an incredible leadership coach, for our conversations about leadership throughout my writing journey. You can discover Jon's virtues at linkedin.com/in/jon-eddy-4470963.

Writing about deeply personal experiences isn't easy, and someone had to keep me sane along the way—thank you, Anne Ligthart, for doing exactly that and so much more. I literally thank you for my sanity. (www.2ndopinionpsychotherapy.com)

GRATITUDE

Fiona Wainrit, career coach extraordinaire (www.careermojo.com.au), is the one who gave me the nudge (more like a big loving push) to finally write this book. I am so grateful for your unwavering belief in me and your encouragement. You also introduced me to the amazing Julie Postance (www.juliepostance.com) before I even put pen to paper. I could not have done this without Julie, the self-publishing guru (and I do mean *guru*); you made this journey lighter, easier, and wonderfully possible. In turn, Julie introduced me to Sophie White and Cortni Merritt whose kindness, patience and guidance to get this book across the line was humbling.

A big glass is raised to my best buddies for life—Pauline White and Caroline Roach—reviewers, critics, wine drinkers, and thought partners. Thank you for the countless phone calls, for listening, for drinking with me, and for reading, rereading, and re-rereading. I love you both dearly.

And to my beautiful Lydia—there aren't enough words to capture how big my heart is when I think of you and how grateful I am to be your mum. Thank you for keeping it real, as always.

Finally, thank you to the lady who answered Lifeline that night.

References

Books

Bunting, Michael, and Lemieux, Carl. 2023. *Vertical Growth: How Self-Awareness Transforms Leaders and Teams*. John Wiley & Sons.

Eddy, Bill. 2018. *Five Types of People That Can Ruin Your Life*, 11th ed. Tarcherperigee.

Kirby, Dean. 2024. *Angel Meadow: Victorian Britain's Most Savage Slum*, 5th ed. Pen & Sword History.

Lencioni, Patrick. 2002. *The Five Dysfunctions of a Team*. Jossey-Bass.

Articles

Baer, Markus, and Frese, Michael. 2003. "Innovation is not enough: climates for initiative and psychological safety, process innovations, and firm performance." *Journal of Organizational Behavior* 24 (1): 45–68. doi:10.1002/job.179

Carmeli, Abraham, Reiter-Palmon, Roni, and Ziv, Enbal. 2010. "Inclusive Leadership and Employee Involvement in Creative Tasks in the Workplace: The Mediating Role of Psychological Safety." *Creativity Research Journal 22 (3): 250–260*. doi:10.1080/10400419.2010.504654. ISSN 1040-0419. S2CID 40912227.

Kim Sehoon, Lee Heesu, and Connerton Timothy. P. July 24, 2020. "How Psychological Safety Affects Team Performance: Mediating Role of Efficacy and Learning Behavior." *Frontiers in Psychology*. 11–1581. doi: 10.3389/fpsyg.2020.01581.

Patil, Rajeshwari, Raheja, Deepali, Nair, Lakshmi, Deshpande, Amruta, and Mittal, Amit. 2023. "The Power of Psychological Safety: Investigating its Impact on Team Learning, Team Efficacy, and Team Productivity." *Open Psychology Journal*, 16: e187435012307090. http://dx.doi.org/10.2174/18743501-v16-230727-2023-36.

REFERENCES

Websites

Bauck, Whitney, Fashionista. January 17, 2019. "Patagonia's CEO on How Saving the Planet Has Been Good for Business." https://fashionista.com/2019/01/patagonia-politics-ceo-rose-marcario-interview.

Capelli, Peter. November 21, 2023. "The Downside of Psychological Safety in the Workplace." Knowledge at Wharton. https://knowledge.wharton.upenn.edu/article/the-downside-of-psychological-safety-in-the-workplace/.

Cherry, Kendra. June 26, 2024. "The Pros and Cons Laissez-Faire Leadership." Very Well Mind. https://www.verywellmind.com/what-is-laissez-faire-leadership-2795316.

Cherry, Kendra. February 7, 2025. "Situational Leadership Theory." Very Well Mind. https://www.verywellmind.com/what-is-the-situational-theory-of-leadership-2795321.

Clear, James. *n.d.* "Core Values List." Accessed March 18, 2025. https://jamesclear.com/core-values.

Claes-Mikael Ståhl. April 3, 2023. "Stress at Work: Countering Europe's New Pandemic." Social Europe. https://www.socialeurope.eu/stress-at-work-countering-europes-new-pandemic.

Cook, Brier. November 22, 2022. "The 5 Levels of Listening as a Leadership Tool." Fellow. https://fellow.app/blog/leadership/the-levels-of-listening-as-a-leadership-tool/.

Craig, Heather. January 30, 2019. "Emotional Intelligence Theories & Components Explained." PositivePsychology.com. https://positivepsychology.com/emotional-intelligence-theories/.

Cutting Edge PR. December 11, 2024. "How to Motivate People to Offer More Constructive Dissent in Meetings." https://cuttingedgepr.com/articles/how-to-motivate-people-to-offer-more-constructive-dissent-at-meetings/.

Davis, Jess. July 3, 2018. "How the AWB Oil-for-Food Scandal Changed Australia's Wheat Industry: 10 Years Since Deregulation." https://www.abc.net.au/news/rural/2018-07-04/awb-deregulation-10-years-after-oil-for-food-scandal/9935308.

The Decision Lab. *n.d.* "The Leader-Member Exchange Theory." Accessed March 9, 2025. https://thedecisionlab.com/reference-guide/management/the-leader-member-exchange-theory.

Dressler, David. February 15, 2024. "4 Elements of Heart-Centered Leadership (and why they matter, especially now)." Medium. https://davidtdressler.medium.com/4-elements-of-heart-centered-leadership-and-why-they-matter-especially-now-ec9d050f8d41.

Elkin, Rachel. November 20, 2022. "Workplace Bullying: What Is It and How Do We Stop It." PsychiatryUK. https://psychiatry-uk.com/workplace-bullying-what-is-it-and-how-do-we-stop-it.

Evans, Joshua. *n.d.* "Leadership Blog." Accessed February 7 2025. https://joshuamevans.com/blog/.

Faraci, Margot. 2023. "Love Leadership Survey." https://www.margotfaraci.com/loveleadershipsurvey.

Field Notes. June 30, 2022. "The Command-and-Control Hangover." https://admiredleadership-wp.carney.co/field-notes/the-command-and-control-hangover/.

Gallup. 2023. "World Risk Poll 2021: Safe at Work? Global Experiences of Violence and Harassment." https://www.lrfoundation.org.uk/sites/default/files/2024-06/LRF_2021_report_safe-at-work.pdf.

Gardner, Kyra. *n.d.* "Heart-Centered Leadership as a Path Forward." Ellevate. Accessed May 16, 2025. https://www.ellevatenetwork.com/articles/12236-heart-centered-leadership-as-a-path-forward.

Geraghty, Tom. December 10, 2020. "Psychological Safety, Diversity & Inclusion." Psych Safety by Iterum. https://psychsafety.com/psychological-safety-inclusion-and-political-beliefs/.

Google re:Work, "Understand team effectiveness." Accessed March 24, 2025. https://rework.withgoogle.com/en/guides/understanding-team-effectiveness.

Harding, Dee. July 10, 2012. "Leading with Heart Centred Emotional Intelligence - Dee Harding." The Coaching Academy. https://www.the-coaching-academy.com/blog/2012/07/leading-with-heart-centered-emotional-intelligence-dee-harding-403.

REFERENCES

Kizilkan, Katrin. Flair HR. January 22, 2024. "180 Leadership Statistics: Training, Challenges, and More." https://flair.hr/en/blog/leadership-statistics/.

Leader Factor. January 27, 2025. "Psychological Safety: The Model by Timothy R. Clark." https://www.leaderfactor.com/learn/psychological-safety-timothy-clark.

Leaders Edge. February 17, 2025. "Heart-Centered Leadership: A Game Changer for Your Team and You." https://www.leadersedgeinc.com/blog/heart-centered-leadership-a-game-changer-for-your-team-and-you?.

Lehman, Katelyn. September 20, 2024. "Heart-Centered Leadership: Cultivating a Just, Equitable, Diverse and Inclusive World." Medium. https://medium.com/illumination/heart-centered-leadership-cultivating-a-just-equitable-diverse-and-inclusive-world-a909a0f526b1.

McEwen, Kathryn. 2018. "Resilience at Work: A Framework for Coaching and Interventions." https://www.workingwithresilience.com.au/wp-content/uploads/2018/09/Whitepaper-Sept18.pdf.

PROSCI. n.d. "The PROSCI ADKAR Model." Accessed March 17, 2025. https://www.prosci.com/methodology/adkar.

The Recovery Village. August 30, 2024. "Narcissistic Personality Disorder Statistics & Prevalence Rates." https://www.therecoveryvillage.com/mental-health/narcissistic-personality-disorder/npd-statistics/.

Robinson, Cheryl. December 4, 2024. "Imposter Syndrome: Genuine Psychological Phenomenon Or An Excuse?" *Forbes*. https://www.forbes.com/sites/cherylrobinson/2024/12/04/imposter-syndrome-genuine-psychological-phenomenon-or-an-excuse/.

Schooley, Skye. July 26, 2024. "Workplace Bullying: How to Identify and Handle It." Business.com. https://www.business.com/articles/the-cold-hard-facts-about-workplace-bullying-and-how-to-handle-it/.

Setyan, S. December 31, 2023. "Workplace Harassment Statistics in 2023." Setyan Law NPC. https://setyanlaw.com/workplace-harassment-statistics-in-2023/.

Skillicorn, Nick. January 4, 2022. "These Companies Failed Because

Leaders Did not Want to Hear Bad News: The Ostrich Effect." Idea to Value. https://www.ideatovalue.com/inno/nickskillicorn/2022/01/these-companies-failed-because-leaders-did-not-want-to-hear-bad-news-the-ostrich-effect/.

Sunovieri, Cherie. June 28, 2022. "Followership: What It Is and Why It's Essential for Leaders to Understand." Bethel University. https://www.bethel.edu/blog/followership/.

Tremlett, Giles. March 7, 2013. "Mondragon: Spain's Giant Co-operative Where Times Are Hard but Few Go Bust." The Guardian. https://www.theguardian.com/world/2013/mar/07/mondragon-spains-giant-cooperative.

Villars Institute. September 25, 2023. "Five Traits to Look for in a System's Leader." https://villarsinstitute.org/posts/five-traits-to-look-for-in-a-systems-leader.

Voltage Control. May 20, 2024. "Safe Collaboration: Managing Conflict and Fostering Dissent." https://voltagecontrol.com/articles/safe-collaboration-managing-conflict-fostering-dissent/.

WomensMedia. January 2, 2022. "5 Ways Post-Traumatic Growth Helps You Recover with Resilience." *Forbes*. https://www.forbes.com/sites/womensmedia/2022/01/02/5-ways-post-traumatic-growth-helps-you-recover-with-resilience/.

World Economic Forum. September 24, 2019. "Systems Leadership Can Change the World—but What Exactly Is It?" https://www.weforum.org/stories/2019/09/systems-leadership-can-change-the-world-but-what-does-it-mean/.

Glossary of Terms

Accountability	*Being responsible for what you do and able to give a satisfactory reason for it.*
Adaptability	*Being able to adjust to new conditions.*
Adaptive Leadership	*Leadership style that emphasizes mobilizing groups to handle tough challenges and moving beyond traditional top-down leadership.*
Adversity	*A state of serious or continued difficulty or misfortune.*
Authenticity	*Being genuine or real.*
Authoritarian	*Enforcing strict obedience to authority at the expense of personal freedom.*
Authorizing Environment	*The formal and informal people, processes, and systems that grant legitimacy to act, make decisions, and implement.*
Bullying	*Seeking to harm. Intimidate, or coerce someone who is perceived as vulnerable.*
Burn out	*A state of emotional, physical, and mental exhaustion caused by excessive and prolonged stress.*
Collaboration	*The action of working with someone to produce something.*
Compassion	*Sympathetic pity and concern for the sufferings or misfortunes of others.*
Constructive Dissent	*The practice of encouraging open, respectful debate within the workplace.*
Control	*The power to influence or direct people's behavior or the course of events.*
Demotivate	*Make someone less eager to work or study.*
Dignity	*Being worthy of honor or respect.*
Discrimination	*Treating someone differently from others.*

Diversity	Having a range of people from varying backgrounds and various lifestyles, experiences, and interests.
Empathy	Understanding and responding appropriately to the feelings of others.
Emotional Intelligence	The ability to recognize, understand, and manage our own emotions while effectively responding to the emotions of others.
Empowerment	Providing people with the authority, confidence, and support needed to make decisions and own their work.
Exclusion	The act of prohibiting someone or something from taking part in an activity or entering a place.
Followership	How individuals respond to and interact with their leader and manager.
Gaslighting	A psychological manipulation technique in which a person tries to convince someone that their reality is untrue.
Genuineness	Being real and exactly what something appears to be.
Humiliation	The embarrassment and shame you feel when someone makes you appear incompetent, or when you make a mistake in public.
Humility	Having a modest or low view of one's importance.
Image Management	Referring to the time and energy we waste in organizations on blame, denial, deflection, defense, gossiping, politics, saving face, masking our weaknesses, and other fear-based strategies to make ourselves feel safe or look good.
Imposter Syndrome	The persistent inability to believe that one's success is deserved or has been legitimately achieved as a result of one's own efforts or skills.

GLOSSARY OF TERMS

Inclusion	The practice of providing equal access to opportunities and resources for people who might otherwise be excluded or marginalized.
Individual Contributor	An employee who works independently and contributes to a team without managing others.
In-Group/Out-Group	An in-group to which a person identifies as being a member. An out-group is a group with which an individual does not identify.
Innovation	The process of introducing new ideas, methods, products, or services that significantly improve or advance an organization.
Integrity	The quality of being honest and having strong moral principles.
Kindness	The quality of being friendly, generous, and considerate.
Laissez-Faire Leadership	A philosophy or practice characterized by a usually deliberate abstention from direction or interference especially with individual freedom of choice and action.
Lived Experience	An individual's personal and subjective encounters, including emotions, perceptions, and knowledge gained through direct, first-hand involvement in everyday events.
Micromanagement	A leadership style that involves excessive control and attention to detail.
Misogyny	Dislike of, contempt for, or ingrained prejudice against women.
Motivated	Has a reason for doing something.
Narcissism	A personality trait or disorder that involves an exaggerated sense of self-importance, a lack of empathy, and a need for admiration.

Narcissistic Personality Disorder	*A mental health condition characterized by an inflated sense of self-importance, a deep need for admiration, and a lack of empathy for others.*
Ostrich Effect	*The Ostrich Effect happens when leaders actively avoid bad news.*
Out-Group/In-Group	*An in-group to which a person identifies as being a member. An out-group is a group with which an individual does not identify.*
Psychological Safety	*A shared belief that an environment is safe for interpersonal risk-taking. In simple terms, it means people can ask questions, share concerns, admit mistakes, and experiment without fear of humiliation or punishment.*
Resilience	*The process and outcome of successfully adapting to difficult or challenging life experiences, especially mental, emotional, and behavioral.*
Respect	*Valuing people's contributions, ideas, and individuality.*
Self-awareness	*Understanding your own thoughts, feelings, and actions.*
Self-regulation	*Managing your emotions in a constructive way.*
Service	*The mindset that leadership is about uplifting, guiding, and empowering others.*
Situational Leadership	*A leadership style that involves adapting your approach to the situation and the people you are leading.*
Social Skills	*Interacting well with other people, being able to clearly articulate thoughts while actively listening.*
Support	*The structure that enables people to grow, experiment, and reach their potential.*

GLOSSARY OF TERMS

Systems Leadership	*An overarching approach to leadership that recognizes the collective rather than the individual.*
Toxicity	*Being harmful or unpleasant in a pervasive or insidious way.*
Toxic Leadership	*A pattern of behavior that harms employees and the organization.*
Transparency	*Sharing thoughts and opinions honestly and respectfully.*
Trauma	*A deeply distressing or disturbing experience.*
Trust	*Being able to believe in the honesty and reliability of someone.*
Uncomfortable	*Feeling unease or awkwardness.*
Unmotivated	*Not having interest in or enthusiasm for something.*
Vulnerability	*Being exposed to the possibility of being hurt or attacked.*
Workplace Culture	*The shared values, beliefs, and behaviors that define an organization's work environment.*
Walk the Talk	*Put words into actions to show that you mean what you say.*

Would You Like to Work with Jane?

If you've made it this far, thank you so much. Writing this book has been one of the most vulnerable, empowering, and heart-opening things I've ever done—and if something in these pages resonated with you, I want you to know: you're not alone, and you don't have to figure it all out by yourself.

I work with individuals and leadership teams who are ready to explore a different way of leading—one that is grounded in emotional intelligence, psychological safety, and connection. Whether you're beginning your leadership journey or navigating a change at a senior level, I offer

- one-on-one leadership coaching and mentoring
- heart-centered leadership workshops for teams
- speaking engagements and podcast interviews

For organizations looking to improve their culture—let's talk about consulting tailored to fit your needs.

If you're curious about working together or are interested in sharing what this book sparked for you, I'd love to hear from you.

Email: pjanep@gmail.com
Instagram: @janephippsauthor
www.theheart-centeredleader.com
linkedin.com/in/janephipps

www.ingramcontent.com/pod-product-compliance
Lightning Source LLC
Chambersburg PA
CBHW061727070526
44583CB00024B/3041